Mystery Mu 103 Wholesome Recipes Inspired by Scooby-Doo

Cream Colombia Ajiaco Chicken

Copyright © 2023 Cream Colombia Ajiaco Chicken
All rights reserved.

Contents

INTRODUCTION 8

1. Scooby Snacks 10
2. Mystery Machine Munchies 11
3. Shaggy's Sandwich Surprise 13
4. Velma's Veggie Delight 14
5. Daphne's Dazzling Fruit Platter 16
6. Fred's Fruit Kabobs 17
7. Haunted Hot Dogs 19
8. Creepy Crawly Cupcakes 20
9. Spooky Spiderweb Pizza 22
10. Ghostly Grilled Cheese 24
11. Werewolf Waffles 25
12. Mummy Mac 'n' Cheese 26
13. Frankenberry Cereal Parfait 28
14. Zombie Ziti 30
15. Vampire Vegetarian Chili 32
16. Goblin Granola Bars 33
17. Ghoulish Green Smoothie 35
18. Phantom Popcorn 36
19. Swampy S'mores 38
20. Monster Meatball Sliders 40
21. Shiver Shake 41
22. Witches' Brew Punch 43
23. Goblin Goulash 44
24. Eerie Eyeball Cake Pops 46
25. Specter Spinach Dip 48
26. Ghostly Guacamole 49
27. Bat Bites 51

28. Enchanted Edamame 52
29. Jack-O'-Lantern Jello 54
30. Devilish Deviled Eggs 55
31. Zombie Zone Nachos 57
32. Mysterious Meringue Cookies 58
33. Cursed Carrot Sticks 60
34. Pumpkin Patch Pudding 61
35. Haunted Hash Browns 63
36. Poltergeist Peanut Butter Cups 65
37. Abominable Apple Pie 67
38. Batty Banana Bread 68
39. Mummy Mocha Latte 70
40. Wacky Witch Fingers (Cheese Sticks) 71
41. Goblin Grapes 73
42. Phantom Pita Chips 74
43. Wicked Watermelon Slices 76
44. Shaggy's Scooby-Doo Stew 77
45. Velma's Veggie Wraps 79
46. Daphne's Delicate Dessert Crepes 80
47. Fred's Fruit Salsa 82
48. Haunted Hamburger Sliders 83
49. Creepy Crawly Rice Krispies Treats 85
50. Ghostly Gingerbread Cookies 86
51. Werewolf Walnut Brownies 88
52. Mummy Meatball Subs 90
53. Frankenfruit Salad 91
54. Zombie Zucchini Muffins 93
55. Vampire Vanilla Cupcakes 94
56. Goblin Gazpacho 96

57. Ghoulish Greek Yogurt Parfait..98
58. Phantom Pumpkin Soup..99
59. Swampy Spinach Artichoke Dip...101
60. Monster Mash Mashed Potatoes..103
61. Shiver-inducing Sherbet..104
62. Witches' Whirlwind Wraps...106
63. Goblin Gingersnap Cookies...108
64. Ectoplasmic Energy Bars..109
65. Spectral Strawberry Shortcake..111
66. Ghostly Garlic Bread..113
67. Bat Berry Smoothie Bowl..114
68. Enchanted Egg Salad...116
69. Jack-O'-Lantern Jalapeño Poppers..117
70. Devilishly Dark Chocolate Fondue..119
71. Zombie Zoodle Salad..120
72. Mysterious Maple Glazed Carrots...122
73. Hauntingly Healthy Hummus...123
74. Poltergeist Pumpkin Pie...125
75. Abominable Avocado Toast...126
76. Batty Blueberry Muffins..128
77. Mummy Mango Salsa..130
78. Wicked Walnut Trail Mix..131
79. Mocha Monster Brownie Bites...133
80. Wacky Watercress Wraps...134
81. Goblin Gravy...136
82. Phantom Pesto Pasta..137
83. Shaggy's Sweet Potato Fries..139
84. Velma's Vanilla Yogurt Parfait..141
85. Daphne's Dill Pickle Spears..142

86. Fred's Fiesta Quesadillas 144
87. Haunted Honeydew Skewers 146
88. Creepy Cauliflower Bites 147
89. Ghostly Gorgonzola Dip 149
90. Werewolf Walnut Trail Mix 150
91. Mummy Mango Smoothie 152
92. Frankenberry French Toast 153
93. Zombie Zoodle Stir-Fry 155
94. Vampire Vanilla Pudding 157
95. Goblin Garlic Knots 158
96. Ghoulish Grilled Pineapple 160
97. Phantom Peach Cobbler 161
98. Swampy Strawberry Salad 163
99. Monster Macadamia Nut Cookies 165
100. Shiver-inducing Shrimp Cocktail 166
101. Witches' Walnut Pesto 168
102. Goblin Green Bean Almondine 170
103. Ectoplasmic Edamame Dip 171
CONCLUSION 174

INTRODUCTION

Welcome to the culinary world of "Mystery Munchies: 103 Wholesome Recipes Inspired by Scooby-Doo." In this enchanting cookbook, we embark on a gastronomic journey that transcends the realms of mystery and nostalgia, bringing to life the delectable delights that have fueled the adventures of everyone's favorite canine detective, Scooby-Doo, and his gang of intrepid friends.

Scooby-Doo, the iconic Great Dane with an insatiable appetite for both food and mystery, has been an integral part of our lives for decades. Whether it's unmasking villains or satisfying his colossal hunger, Scooby-Doo's adventures have left an indelible mark on pop culture. And what better way to celebrate this timeless character than by creating a collection of 103 recipes inspired by the delectable delights that have graced the screen alongside our beloved Mystery Inc.?

In "Mystery Munchies," each recipe is a culinary tribute to the whimsical world of Scooby-Doo, offering a delightful fusion of flavors, creativity, and a dash of nostalgia. From hearty sandwiches that could rival Scooby and Shaggy's infamous stacked subs to sweet treats inspired by the colorful villains encountered on their mystery-solving escapades, this cookbook is a treasure trove of mouthwatering concoctions designed to bring joy to Scooby-Doo fans young and old.

The inspiration for these recipes comes not just from the iconic moments in the animated series but also from the diverse array of settings the Mystery Inc. gang finds themselves in. Whether it's a spooky haunted mansion, a carnival filled with peculiar characters, or a beachside snack shack, each locale has contributed its unique flavor to the culinary creations within these pages.

Dive into the world of Scooby-Doo as you recreate the gang's favorite meals while solving culinary mysteries of your own. From Scooby Snacks that will have you exclaiming, "Scooby-Dooby-Doo, where are you?" to hearty meals that capture the essence of those late-night stakeouts, "Mystery Munchies" ensures that every recipe is crafted with love and a touch of mystery.

This cookbook isn't just a collection of recipes; it's a nostalgic voyage through the annals of Scooby-Doo history. Imagine preparing a meal inspired by the gang's favorite hangout, the Mystery Machine, or crafting a dessert that mirrors the vibrant colors of the classic villains' disguises. "Mystery Munchies" is more than a cookbook; it's a culinary adventure that invites you to relive the magic of Scooby-Doo in your own kitchen.

So, grab your apron, gather your ingredients, and get ready to embark on a culinary quest that pays homage to the enduring charm of Scooby-Doo and his friends. "Mystery Munchies" is not just about food; it's about creating memories, sharing laughs, and indulging in the whimsy that makes Scooby-Doo an eternal favorite. Get ready for a gastronomic journey where every recipe tells a story, and every bite is a taste of nostalgia.

1. Scooby Snacks

Embark on a culinary adventure with these homemade Scooby Snacks inspired by everyone's favorite mystery-solving Great Dane and his gang! These delightful treats are perfect for any Scooby-Doo fan, whether you're hosting a themed party or just craving a nostalgic snack. Packed with flavor and a hint of mystery, these Scooby Snacks are sure to be a hit at your next gathering.

Serving: Makes approximately 24 Scooby Snacks
Preparation Time: 15 minutes
Ready Time: 30 minutes

Ingredients:
- 2 cups old-fashioned rolled oats
- 1 cup creamy peanut butter
- 1/2 cup honey
- 1 teaspoon vanilla extract
- 1/2 cup chocolate chips
- 1/2 cup shredded coconut (optional)
- 1/4 cup chopped nuts (walnuts or almonds work well)
- Pinch of salt

Instructions:
1. In a large mixing bowl, combine the rolled oats, peanut butter, honey, and vanilla extract. Stir until well combined.
2. Add the chocolate chips, shredded coconut (if using), chopped nuts, and a pinch of salt to the mixture. Mix thoroughly to ensure even distribution of ingredients.
3. Line a baking sheet with parchment paper.
4. Scoop out small portions of the mixture and roll them into bite-sized balls. Place the balls on the prepared baking sheet, leaving some space between each.
5. Using the back of a fork, gently press down on each ball to create a crisscross pattern, giving them the classic Scooby Snack appearance.
6. Place the baking sheet in the refrigerator for at least 15 minutes to allow the Scooby Snacks to set.

7. Once set, transfer the Scooby Snacks to an airtight container and store in the refrigerator until ready to serve.

Nutrition Information:
(Per serving - 1 Scooby Snack)
- Calories: 120
- Total Fat: 7g
- Saturated Fat: 2g
- Cholesterol: 0mg
- Sodium: 50mg
- Total Carbohydrates: 12g
- Dietary Fiber: 2g
- Sugars: 6g
- Protein: 3g

Enjoy these Scooby Snacks as a tasty and wholesome treat that captures the essence of mystery-solving fun!

2. Mystery Machine Munchies

Embark on a culinary adventure with the "Mystery Machine Munchies," inspired by the iconic Scooby-Doo and the gang. These munchies are a delightful blend of flavors and textures, perfect for satisfying your appetite as you solve mysteries or simply enjoy a nostalgic meal. Gather your friends, fire up the Mystery Machine, and get ready to indulge in these scrumptious treats!

Serving: Makes approximately 20 munchies
Preparation Time: 15 minutes
Ready Time: 30 minutes

Ingredients:
- 2 cups shredded cooked chicken
- 1 cup shredded cheddar cheese
- 1/2 cup diced tomatoes
- 1/4 cup diced red onions
- 1/4 cup diced green bell pepper
- 1/4 cup sliced black olives
- 1/4 cup chopped fresh cilantro

- 1 teaspoon ground cumin
- 1 teaspoon chili powder
- 1/2 teaspoon garlic powder
- Salt and pepper to taste
- 20 small flour tortillas
- Cooking spray

Instructions:
1. Preheat your oven to 375°F (190°C).
2. In a large mixing bowl, combine the shredded chicken, cheddar cheese, tomatoes, red onions, green bell pepper, black olives, and cilantro.
3. Add the ground cumin, chili powder, garlic powder, salt, and pepper to the mixture. Mix everything thoroughly until well combined.
4. Place a small amount of the mixture onto each flour tortilla, then fold the tortillas in half, creating a half-moon shape. Press the edges to seal.
5. Lightly spray a baking sheet with cooking spray. Arrange the filled tortillas on the sheet, ensuring they are not touching.
6. Bake in the preheated oven for 15-20 minutes or until the munchies are golden brown and crispy.
7. Remove from the oven and let them cool for a few minutes before serving.

Nutrition Information:
(Per serving, based on 4 munchies)
- Calories: 320
- Total Fat: 15g
- Saturated Fat: 6g
- Cholesterol: 45mg
- Sodium: 580mg
- Total Carbohydrates: 28g
- Dietary Fiber: 2g
- Sugars: 2g
- Protein: 18g

These Mystery Machine Munchies are sure to be a hit at any gathering. Enjoy the combination of savory chicken, melted cheese, and vibrant vegetables, wrapped in a crispy tortilla. It's a snack worthy of any Scooby-Doo mystery-solving celebration!

3. Shaggy's Sandwich Surprise

Step into the whimsical world of Scooby-Doo with "Shaggy's Sandwich Surprise" – a mouthwatering creation inspired by the legendary appetite of Shaggy Rogers. This sandwich is a delightful medley of flavors and textures that promises to satisfy even the heartiest of appetites. Packed with ingredients that would make Scooby and the gang proud, this sandwich is a perfect addition to your Scooby-Doo-inspired culinary adventures.

Serving: 4 servings
Preparation Time: 15 minutes
Ready Time: 15 minutes

Ingredients:
- 1 pound deli-sliced turkey
- 1/2 pound sliced Swiss cheese
- 8 slices whole wheat bread
- 1 cup baby spinach leaves
- 1 large tomato, thinly sliced
- 1/2 red onion, thinly sliced
- 1/4 cup mayonnaise
- 2 tablespoons Dijon mustard
- 1 tablespoon honey
- 1 teaspoon dried oregano
- Salt and pepper to taste
- 4 tablespoons butter, softened

Instructions:
1. Prepare the Spread:
In a small bowl, mix together mayonnaise, Dijon mustard, honey, and dried oregano. Set aside.
2. Build the Sandwich:
Lay out 8 slices of whole wheat bread. On 4 slices, layer deli-sliced turkey, Swiss cheese, spinach leaves, tomato slices, and red onion. Season with salt and pepper to taste.
3. Spread the Sauce:
Generously spread the prepared mayonnaise mixture on the remaining 4 slices of bread. Place these slices on top of the assembled ingredients to create sandwiches.

4. Butter and Grill:
Lightly butter the outer sides of each sandwich. Heat a skillet or griddle over medium heat. Grill the sandwiches on each side until the bread is golden brown, and the cheese is melted, approximately 3-4 minutes per side.

5. Serve:
Remove the sandwiches from the heat, let them cool for a minute, and then slice them in half diagonally. Serve warm and enjoy the Scooby-Doo magic!

Nutrition Information:
(Per serving)
- Calories: 540
- Total Fat: 28g
- Saturated Fat: 12g
- Trans Fat: 0g
- Cholesterol: 90mg
- Sodium: 1100mg
- Total Carbohydrates: 46g
- Dietary Fiber: 6g
- Sugars: 11g
- Protein: 28g

Note: Nutrition information is approximate and may vary based on specific ingredients and portion sizes. Adjust quantities to meet dietary preferences and restrictions.

4. Velma's Veggie Delight

Step into the world of mystery and munchies with Velma's Veggie Delight! Inspired by the brainy and health-conscious Velma Dinkley from Scooby-Doo, this dish is a delightful blend of fresh vegetables and savory flavors. Packed with nutrients and a touch of detective spirit, it's a wholesome treat that even the pickiest eaters will love.

Serving: 4 servings
Preparation Time: 15 minutes
Ready Time: 30 minutes

Ingredients:
- 2 cups broccoli florets
- 1 cup sliced carrots
- 1 cup cherry tomatoes, halved
- 1 bell pepper, thinly sliced (any color)
- 1 zucchini, sliced
- 1 cup snap peas, trimmed
- 1/4 cup olive oil
- 2 cloves garlic, minced
- 1 teaspoon dried oregano
- 1 teaspoon dried basil
- Salt and pepper to taste
- 1/2 cup feta cheese, crumbled (optional)

Instructions:
1. Preheat the oven to 400°F (200°C).
2. In a large mixing bowl, combine broccoli, carrots, cherry tomatoes, bell pepper, zucchini, and snap peas.
3. In a small bowl, whisk together olive oil, minced garlic, oregano, basil, salt, and pepper.
4. Drizzle the olive oil mixture over the vegetables and toss until evenly coated.
5. Spread the vegetables on a baking sheet in a single layer.
6. Roast in the preheated oven for 15-20 minutes or until the vegetables are tender and slightly browned, stirring halfway through.
7. Remove from the oven and sprinkle with crumbled feta cheese if desired.
8. Serve hot as a standalone dish or pair it with your favorite protein.

Nutrition Information:
Note: Nutrition information is approximate and may vary based on specific ingredients and serving sizes.
- Calories: 180 per serving
- Protein: 5g
- Carbohydrates: 15g
- Dietary Fiber: 4g
- Sugars: 6g
- Fat: 12g
- Saturated Fat: 3g
- Cholesterol: 10mg

- Sodium: 200mg

Velma's Veggie Delight is not only a treat for your taste buds but also a nutritious addition to your Scooby-Doo-inspired culinary adventures. Enjoy the mystery-solving goodness in every bite!

5. Daphne's Dazzling Fruit Platter

Step into the world of mystery and deliciousness with Daphne's Dazzling Fruit Platter, a vibrant and refreshing dish inspired by the glamorous and adventurous Daphne Blake from Scooby-Doo. This fruit platter is not only a feast for the eyes but also a nutritious treat that will leave you feeling energized and ready for the next mystery-solving adventure.

Serving: Serves 4-6
Preparation Time: 15 minutes
Ready Time: 15 minutes

Ingredients:
- 1 ripe pineapple, peeled and sliced
- 2 cups strawberries, hulled and halved
- 2 cups green grapes, washed and stemmed
- 2 cups red grapes, washed and stemmed
- 2 kiwi fruits, peeled and sliced
- 1 cup blueberries, washed
- 1 cup blackberries, washed
- 1 mango, peeled and sliced
- 1/2 cup pomegranate seeds
- 1/4 cup fresh mint leaves, for garnish

Instructions:
1. Arrange the pineapple slices in the center of a large serving platter, creating a sunburst pattern.
2. Surround the pineapple with concentric circles of strawberries, green grapes, red grapes, kiwi slices, mango slices, blueberries, and blackberries.
3. Sprinkle pomegranate seeds over the entire platter, adding a burst of color and sweetness.
4. Garnish with fresh mint leaves for a touch of brightness and aroma.

5. Serve immediately and watch as your guests are dazzled by the beauty of this fruit platter inspired by Daphne's style.

Nutrition Information:
Note: Nutrition information is approximate and may vary based on specific ingredients and quantities used.
- Calories: 120 per serving
- Total Fat: 0.5g
- Cholesterol: 0mg
- Sodium: 5mg
- Total Carbohydrates: 30g
- Dietary Fiber: 5g
- Sugars: 22g
- Protein: 2g

Unveil the mystery of a healthy and delicious snack with Daphne's Dazzling Fruit Platter – a delightful addition to your Scooby-Doo inspired culinary journey!

6. Fred's Fruit Kabobs

Indulge your taste buds in a culinary adventure with Fred's Fruit Kabobs, a vibrant and wholesome treat inspired by the colorful and exciting world of Scooby-Doo. These delightful kabobs are not only a feast for the eyes but also a healthy and delicious snack that will satisfy your sweet cravings. Assemble these fruity skewers with a dash of Scooby-Doo flair and bring a burst of flavor to your next gathering. Get ready for a taste sensation that even the Mystery Inc. gang would approve of!

Serving: Makes approximately 6 fruit kabobs.
Preparation Time: 15 minutes
Ready Time: 15 minutes

Ingredients:
- 2 cups fresh pineapple chunks
- 2 cups strawberries, hulled
- 2 cups green grapes
- 1 cup blueberries
- 1 cup mango chunks

- 1 cup kiwi slices
- Wooden skewers

Instructions:
1. Prepare the Fruits:
- Wash and dry all fruits thoroughly.
- Cut the pineapple into bite-sized chunks.
- Hull the strawberries and slice them in half.
- Peel and slice the kiwi into rounds.
- If using whole grapes, wash and pat them dry.
2. Assemble the Kabobs:
- Take a wooden skewer and thread on a combination of fruits, alternating colors for an eye-catching presentation.
- Start with a pineapple chunk, followed by a strawberry half, green grape, blueberry, mango chunk, and kiwi slice.
- Repeat the pattern until the skewer is filled, leaving a bit of space at each end for easy handling.
3. Serve and Enjoy:
- Arrange the fruit kabobs on a serving platter.
- Serve immediately and enjoy the refreshing burst of fruity goodness.

Nutrition Information:
(Per serving, based on 1 kabob)
- Calories: 80
- Total Fat: 0.5g
- Cholesterol: 0mg
- Sodium: 1mg
- Total Carbohydrates: 20g
- Dietary Fiber: 3g
- Sugars: 15g
- Protein: 1g

Note: Nutrition information is approximate and may vary based on the specific fruits used. Adjust quantities according to personal preferences and dietary requirements. Now, embark on a culinary journey inspired by the beloved Scooby-Doo and treat yourself to the goodness of Fred's Fruit Kabobs!

7. Haunted Hot Dogs

Get ready to embark on a spooky culinary adventure with our "Haunted Hot Dogs" recipe, inspired by the iconic mystery-solving gang from Scooby-Doo! These ghoulishly delightful hot dogs are perfect for a Scooby-Doo-themed gathering or any Halloween celebration. The combination of savory hot dogs, gooey cheese, and mysterious toppings will have everyone craving more. So, gather your gang and let's dive into the delicious mystery of Haunted Hot Dogs!

Serving: Serves 6
Preparation Time: 15 minutes
Ready Time: 30 minutes

Ingredients:
- 6 hot dog buns
- 6 beef or vegetarian hot dogs
- 1 cup shredded cheddar cheese
- 1/2 cup diced red onions
- 1/2 cup pickled jalapeños
- 1/4 cup ketchup
- 1/4 cup mustard
- 1 tablespoon olive oil
- Salt and pepper to taste
- 1/4 cup chopped fresh parsley (for garnish)
- 6 slices of American cheese, cut into ghost shapes (optional)

Instructions:
1. Preheat the Grill or Stovetop: If using a grill, preheat it to medium-high heat. If using a stovetop, set a large skillet or grilling pan over medium-high heat.
2. Prepare the Hot Dogs: Brush the hot dogs with olive oil and season with salt and pepper to taste.
3. Grill the Hot Dogs: Place the hot dogs on the preheated grill or in the skillet. Cook for 5-7 minutes, turning occasionally, until they are heated through and have grill marks.
4. Toast the Buns: In the last minute of cooking, place the hot dog buns on the grill or in a separate pan to toast lightly.

5. Assemble the Haunted Hot Dogs: Place a grilled hot dog in each bun. Sprinkle shredded cheddar cheese over the hot dogs, allowing it to melt slightly. Add diced red onions and pickled jalapeños for a spooky kick.
6. Add Condiments: Drizzle ketchup and mustard over the Haunted Hot Dogs to create fun and flavorful designs.
7. Garnish: Sprinkle chopped fresh parsley over the top for a burst of color and freshness. If desired, add ghost-shaped American cheese slices on top.
8. Serve: Arrange the Haunted Hot Dogs on a platter and serve them up to your hungry guests.

Nutrition Information:
Note: Nutritional values may vary based on specific ingredients used.
- Calories: ~350 per serving
- Total Fat: 18g
- Saturated Fat: 8g
- Trans Fat: 0g
- Cholesterol: 40mg
- Sodium: 900mg
- Total Carbohydrates: 32g
- Dietary Fiber: 3g
- Sugars: 6g
- Protein: 15g

Enjoy these Haunted Hot Dogs as a deliciously spooky addition to your Scooby-Doo-inspired feast!

8. Creepy Crawly Cupcakes

'Step into the world of mystery and fun with these 'Creepy Crawly Cupcakes' inspired by Scooby-Doo! Perfect for a spooky party or a fun baking session, these cupcakes will thrill and delight all Scooby-Doo fans with their eerie charm and delicious taste. Get ready to whip up a batch of these treats that are sure to disappear faster than Scooby's snacks!"

Serving: Makes 12 cupcakes
Preparation Time: 20 minutes
Ready Time: 45 minutes

Ingredients:

For the cupcakes:
- 1 and 1/2 cups all-purpose flour
- 1 cup granulated sugar
- 1/4 cup unsweetened cocoa powder
- 1 teaspoon baking soda
- 1/2 teaspoon salt
- 1 cup water
- 1/3 cup vegetable oil
- 1 tablespoon white vinegar
- 1 teaspoon vanilla extract

For the frosting and decoration:
- 1/2 cup unsalted butter, softened
- 2 cups powdered sugar
- 2-3 tablespoons milk or cream
- Green food coloring
- Gummy worms
- Edible googly eyes
- Black decorating gel

Instructions:

1. Preheat your oven to 350°F (175°C). Line a cupcake pan with paper liners.
2. In a large mixing bowl, whisk together the flour, sugar, cocoa powder, baking soda, and salt until well combined.
3. Make a well in the center of the dry ingredients and add the water, vegetable oil, vinegar, and vanilla extract. Mix until the batter is smooth and no lumps remain.
4. Fill each cupcake liner about two-thirds full with the batter. Bake in the preheated oven for 18-20 minutes or until a toothpick inserted into the center of a cupcake comes out clean. Remove from the oven and let them cool completely on a wire rack.
5. For the frosting, beat the softened butter in a mixing bowl until creamy. Gradually add the powdered sugar, alternating with the milk or cream, until the frosting reaches a smooth and spreadable consistency. Add green food coloring to achieve the desired spooky hue.
6. Once the cupcakes are cooled, frost them generously with the green frosting using a spatula or piping bag.

7. To create the creepy crawly effect, place gummy worms on top of the frosted cupcakes, letting them peek out and "crawl" across the frosting. Add edible googly eyes to some of the worms for an extra spooky touch.
8. Use black decorating gel to draw squiggly lines or "tracks" around the worms to simulate their movement.

Nutrition Information (per serving):
Calories: 280
Total Fat: 14g
Saturated Fat: 6g
Cholesterol: 25mg
Sodium: 210mg
Total Carbohydrate: 38g
Dietary Fiber: 1g
Sugars: 26g
Protein: 2g
Enjoy these eerie yet delightful Creepy Crawly Cupcakes straight out of the Scooby-Doo universe!

9. Spooky Spiderweb Pizza

In the world of mystery-solving and spooky adventures, Scooby-Doo and the gang have encountered some eerie eats! One dish that captures the essence of their thrilling escapades is the Spooky Spiderweb Pizza. This creative and delicious pizza is perfect for a fun-filled Scooby-Doo themed party or a family movie night. With its eerie appearance and savory taste, it's sure to be a hit among kids and adults alike!

Serving: 4-6 servings
Preparation time: 20 minutes
Ready time: 35 minutes

Ingredients:
- 1 pre-made pizza crust (store-bought or homemade)
- 1 cup pizza sauce
- 2 cups shredded mozzarella cheese
- 1 cup black olives, sliced
- 1 red bell pepper

- Olive oil
- Salt and pepper to taste

Instructions:
1. Preheat your oven to the temperature recommended for your pizza crust.
2. Place the pre-made pizza crust on a baking sheet or pizza stone.
3. Spread the pizza sauce evenly over the crust, leaving a small border around the edges.
4. Sprinkle the shredded mozzarella cheese over the sauce, covering the entire pizza.
5. Create the spiderweb design: Slice the black olives into thin rounds. Place a sliced olive in the center of the pizza. Then, starting from the center, arrange olive slices in a circular pattern, leaving space between each slice to resemble a spiderweb.
6. For the spider: Cut the red bell pepper into small squares or rectangles for the body and legs of the spider. Place the pepper pieces on the pizza near the center, on top of the olive slices, to create a spider shape.
7. Drizzle a small amount of olive oil over the pizza and season with salt and pepper to taste.
8. Place the pizza in the preheated oven and bake according to the crust's instructions or until the cheese is bubbly and golden.
9. Once done, carefully remove the pizza from the oven and let it cool for a few minutes before slicing.

Nutrition Information (per serving, based on 4 servings):
- Calories: 380
- Total Fat: 18g
- Saturated Fat: 8g
- Cholesterol: 40mg
- Sodium: 960mg
- Total Carbohydrate: 37g
- Dietary Fiber: 3g
- Sugars: 4g
- Protein: 17g

Enjoy the eerie delight of the Spooky Spiderweb Pizza while solving mysteries, just like Scooby-Doo and the gang!

10. Ghostly Grilled Cheese

This spooky spin on a classic sandwich is inspired by Scooby-Doo's thrilling adventures. The Ghostly Grilled Cheese is a hauntingly delicious treat that will have you craving more mysteries to solve!

Serving: 2 sandwiches
Preparation time: 10 minutes
Ready time: 20 minutes

Ingredients:
- 4 slices of your favorite bread
- 1 cup shredded mozzarella cheese
- 1 cup shredded cheddar cheese
- 1/4 cup grated Parmesan cheese
- 1/2 teaspoon garlic powder
- 1/2 teaspoon onion powder
- 1/2 teaspoon paprika
- 1/4 teaspoon black pepper
- 4 slices of provolone cheese
- Butter for spreading

Instructions:
1. In a mixing bowl, combine the shredded mozzarella, cheddar, and grated Parmesan cheeses.
2. Add garlic powder, onion powder, paprika, and black pepper to the cheese mixture. Mix well to combine the spices with the cheeses.
3. Butter one side of each slice of bread.
4. Place a slice of provolone cheese on the non-buttered side of two slices of bread.
5. Divide the seasoned cheese mixture evenly between the two slices with the provolone cheese, spreading it evenly.
6. Top each with the remaining two slices of bread, buttered side facing out.
7. Heat a skillet or griddle over medium heat. Carefully transfer the sandwiches onto the skillet.
8. Cook for 3-4 minutes on each side, or until the bread turns golden brown and the cheese melts to oozy perfection.
9. Once both sides are golden and the cheese is melted, remove the sandwiches from the skillet.

10. Let them cool for a minute, then slice each sandwich diagonally.

Nutrition Information (approximate values per serving):
- Calories: 480 kcal
- Fat: 26g
- Saturated Fat: 16g
- Cholesterol: 75mg
- Sodium: 860mg
- Carbohydrates: 34g
- Fiber: 2g
- Sugars: 3g
- Protein: 27g

Enjoy these hauntingly delicious Ghostly Grilled Cheese sandwiches, perfect for a Scooby-Doo-inspired snack or meal!

11. Werewolf Waffles

Step into the mysterious world of Scooby-Doo and his gang with these spooktacular Werewolf Waffles! Inspired by the many creepy encounters and midnight snacks enjoyed by the Mystery Inc. team, these waffles are perfect for breakfast or a midnight snack. The howlingly delicious flavor will have you coming back for more, whether you're solving mysteries or just satisfying your hunger. Get ready to unmask the hunger beast with these irresistible Werewolf Waffles!

Serving: Makes 4 servings.
Preparation Time: 15 minutes.
Ready Time: 25 minutes.

Ingredients:
- 2 cups all-purpose flour
- 2 tablespoons sugar
- 1 tablespoon baking powder
- 1/2 teaspoon salt
- 1 3/4 cups milk
- 1/3 cup vegetable oil
- 2 large eggs
- 1 teaspoon vanilla extract

- 1 cup chocolate chips (for the werewolf eyes)
- Maple syrup and whipped cream (for serving)

Instructions:
1. Preheat your waffle iron according to the manufacturer's instructions.
2. In a large mixing bowl, whisk together the flour, sugar, baking powder, and salt.
3. In a separate bowl, beat together the milk, vegetable oil, eggs, and vanilla extract until well combined.
4. Pour the wet ingredients into the dry ingredients and stir until just combined. Be careful not to overmix; it's okay if there are a few lumps.
5. Pour the batter onto the preheated waffle iron, spreading it evenly. Close the lid and cook until the waffles are golden brown and crisp.
6. While the waffles are cooking, melt the chocolate chips in the microwave or on the stovetop.
7. Once the waffles are done, remove them from the waffle iron and place them on serving plates.
8. Use melted chocolate to create "werewolf eyes" on the waffles. You can make them as spooky or as friendly as you like!
9. Drizzle with maple syrup and top with whipped cream for an extra indulgent treat.

Nutrition Information:
(Per serving)
- Calories: 450
- Fat: 22g
- Cholesterol: 85mg
- Sodium: 520mg
- Carbohydrates: 56g
- Fiber: 2g
- Sugars: 17g
- Protein: 10g

Enjoy your Werewolf Waffles and get ready for a breakfast or snack that's as mysterious and delicious as a Scooby-Doo adventure!

12. Mummy Mac 'n' Cheese

Unravel the mysteries of hunger with our spine-tingling and oh-so-cheesy "Mummy Mac 'n' Cheese," inspired by the iconic Scooby-Doo and the gang! This delightful dish is bound to capture your taste buds in a web of gooey goodness. Perfect for family dinners or spooky gatherings, it's a surefire way to solve the case of the growling stomach!

Serving: Serves 4
Preparation Time: 15 minutes
Ready Time: 40 minutes

Ingredients:
- 2 cups elbow macaroni
- 1/4 cup unsalted butter
- 1/4 cup all-purpose flour
- 1/2 teaspoon salt
- 1/4 teaspoon black pepper
- 1/4 teaspoon garlic powder
- 1/4 teaspoon onion powder
- 2 cups milk
- 2 cups shredded sharp cheddar cheese
- 1 cup shredded mozzarella cheese
- 1/2 cup grated Parmesan cheese
- 8 slices of mummy-shaped string cheese (for topping)

Instructions:
1. Boil the Macaroni:
- Cook the elbow macaroni according to package instructions until al dente. Drain and set aside.
2. Prepare the Cheese Sauce:
- In a saucepan over medium heat, melt the butter. Stir in the flour, salt, pepper, garlic powder, and onion powder until well combined, creating a roux.
- Gradually whisk in the milk, ensuring there are no lumps. Continue to whisk until the mixture thickens, about 5-7 minutes.
- Reduce heat to low, then add the shredded cheddar, mozzarella, and Parmesan cheeses. Stir until the cheese is fully melted and the sauce is smooth.
3. Combine Pasta and Cheese Sauce:
- Add the cooked macaroni to the cheese sauce, stirring until the pasta is evenly coated.

4. Mummify the Mac 'n' Cheese:
- Preheat your oven to 350°F (175°C). Transfer the mac 'n' cheese into a baking dish.
- Take the mummy-shaped string cheese and lay them on top of the mac 'n' cheese to create a whimsical mummy pattern.

5. Bake to Perfection:
- Bake in the preheated oven for 20-25 minutes or until the cheese is bubbly and golden brown.

6. Serve and Enjoy:
- Allow the Mummy Mac 'n' Cheese to cool for a few minutes before serving. Scoop out portions, ensuring each serving has a playful mummy on top.

Nutrition Information (per serving):
- Calories: 480
- Total Fat: 26g
- Saturated Fat: 16g
- Cholesterol: 80mg
- Sodium: 620mg
- Total Carbohydrates: 37g
- Dietary Fiber: 2g
- Sugars: 6g
- Protein: 22g

Unveil the mystery of a delicious meal with this Mummy Mac 'n' Cheese – a perfect homage to Scooby-Doo's endless appetite for fun and flavor!

13. Frankenberry Cereal Parfait

Delve into the whimsical world of Scooby-Doo with this "Frankenberry Cereal Parfait." Inspired by the mysterious and delightful adventures of Scooby and the gang, this parfait brings a playful twist to your breakfast or snack time. Packed with the vibrant flavors of Frankenberry cereal, this treat is a nod to the fun and excitement of solving mysteries with Scooby-Doo.

Serving: Serves 2
Preparation Time: 15 minutes
Ready Time: 15 minutes

Ingredients:
- 2 cups Frankenberry cereal
- 2 cups vanilla yogurt
- 1 cup fresh strawberries, sliced
- 1/2 cup whipped cream
- 1/4 cup chocolate chips
- 2 tablespoons honey
- Mint leaves for garnish (optional)

Instructions:
1. Layering the Base:
- In each serving glass or bowl, start by adding a layer of Frankenberry cereal at the bottom.
2. Yogurt Layer:
- Spoon a generous layer of vanilla yogurt on top of the cereal in each glass.
3. Strawberry Slices:
- Add a layer of fresh strawberry slices on top of the yogurt, distributing them evenly.
4. Repeat Layers:
- Repeat the layers until you reach the top of the glass, finishing with a layer of yogurt.
5. Whipped Cream and Chocolate Chips:
- Dollop whipped cream on the top layer of yogurt and sprinkle chocolate chips over the whipped cream for a delightful crunch.
6. Drizzle with Honey:
- Drizzle honey over the parfait for added sweetness.
7. Garnish (Optional):
- Garnish with mint leaves for a fresh and vibrant touch (optional).
8. Serve:
- Serve immediately and enjoy the playful combination of flavors and textures reminiscent of Scooby-Doo's adventures.

Nutrition Information:
(Per Serving)
- Calories: 400
- Total Fat: 15g
- Saturated Fat: 8g
- Trans Fat: 0g

- Cholesterol: 25mg
- Sodium: 150mg
- Total Carbohydrates: 60g
- Dietary Fiber: 4g
- Sugars: 40g
- Protein: 8g

Note: Nutrition information is approximate and may vary based on specific ingredients used.

14. Zombie Ziti

Embrace the spooky and mysterious world of Scooby-Doo with our "Zombie Ziti" recipe! This eerie dish is inspired by the countless encounters with monsters and ghouls that the Mystery Inc. gang faced during their adventures. The combination of bold flavors and creepy presentation makes this a perfect addition to your Scooby-Doo-inspired cookbook. Get ready to solve the mystery of hunger with this deliciously haunting Zombie Ziti!

Serving: 4-6 servings
Preparation Time: 20 minutes
Ready Time: 45 minutes

Ingredients:
- 1 pound ziti pasta
- 1 tablespoon olive oil
- 1 onion, finely chopped
- 3 cloves garlic, minced
- 1 pound ground beef or ground turkey
- 1 teaspoon dried oregano
- 1 teaspoon dried basil
- 1/2 teaspoon red pepper flakes (adjust to taste)
- Salt and pepper to taste
- 2 cups marinara sauce
- 1 cup ricotta cheese
- 1 cup shredded mozzarella cheese
- 1/2 cup grated Parmesan cheese
- 1 cup black olives, sliced

- Fresh parsley for garnish

Instructions:
1. Preheat your oven to 375°F (190°C).
2. Cook the ziti pasta according to the package instructions. Drain and set aside.
3. In a large skillet, heat olive oil over medium heat. Add chopped onions and minced garlic, sautéing until softened.
4. Add the ground beef or turkey to the skillet, breaking it up with a spoon as it cooks. Cook until browned.
5. Season the meat mixture with dried oregano, dried basil, red pepper flakes, salt, and pepper. Stir well to combine.
6. Pour in the marinara sauce and simmer for 5-7 minutes, allowing the flavors to meld.
7. In a large mixing bowl, combine the cooked ziti with the meat and sauce mixture.
8. In a separate bowl, mix together the ricotta, mozzarella, and Parmesan cheeses.
9. In a baking dish, layer half of the ziti and meat mixture, followed by half of the cheese mixture. Repeat the layers.
10. Arrange sliced black olives on top to create a "zombie" effect.
11. Bake in the preheated oven for 25-30 minutes or until the cheese is melted and bubbly.
12. Garnish with fresh parsley before serving.

Nutrition Information:
(Per Serving - based on 6 servings)
- Calories: 550
- Total Fat: 24g
- Saturated Fat: 10g
- Cholesterol: 85mg
- Sodium: 800mg
- Total Carbohydrates: 49g
- Dietary Fiber: 4g
- Sugars: 6g
- Protein: 32g

Unearth the culinary delights of Scooby-Doo's world with this Zombie Ziti, sure to satisfy both your taste buds and your appetite for mystery!

15. Vampire Vegetarian Chili

Get ready to solve the mystery of hunger with our "Vampire Vegetarian Chili," inspired by the spooky adventures of Scooby-Doo and the gang. Packed with plant-based goodness, this chili is a hearty and satisfying dish that even vampires would sink their fangs into. So, gather your Scooby snacks and prepare to embark on a culinary journey with this ghoulishly delightful recipe!

Serving: Serves 6
Preparation Time: 15 minutes
Ready Time: 1 hour 15 minutes

Ingredients:
- 2 tablespoons olive oil
- 1 large onion, diced
- 3 cloves garlic, minced
- 1 red bell pepper, diced
- 1 green bell pepper, diced
- 1 zucchini, diced
- 1 cup corn kernels (fresh or frozen)
- 2 cans (15 oz each) black beans, drained and rinsed
- 1 can (15 oz) kidney beans, drained and rinsed
- 1 can (28 oz) crushed tomatoes
- 1 cup vegetable broth
- 2 tablespoons tomato paste
- 2 teaspoons ground cumin
- 1 tablespoon chili powder
- 1 teaspoon smoked paprika
- 1/2 teaspoon cayenne pepper (adjust to taste)
- Salt and black pepper to taste
- 1 cup textured vegetable protein (TVP) or cooked lentils (optional)
- Fresh cilantro, chopped (for garnish)
- Vegan cheese, shredded (for topping)

Instructions:
1. Heat olive oil in a large pot over medium heat. Add diced onion and sauté until translucent.
2. Add minced garlic, diced red and green bell peppers, and zucchini to the pot. Cook for 5-7 minutes until vegetables are tender.

3. Stir in corn, black beans, kidney beans, crushed tomatoes, vegetable broth, and tomato paste. Mix well.
4. Season the chili with ground cumin, chili powder, smoked paprika, cayenne pepper, salt, and black pepper. Adjust the seasoning to your taste.
5. If using, add textured vegetable protein (TVP) or cooked lentils to the chili for added protein and texture.
6. Bring the chili to a boil, then reduce the heat to low and let it simmer for 1 hour, stirring occasionally.
7. Once the chili has thickened and flavors have melded together, remove from heat.
8. Serve the Vampire Vegetarian Chili hot, garnished with fresh cilantro and a sprinkle of vegan cheese.

Nutrition Information:
(Per serving)
- Calories: 280
- Total Fat: 6g
- Saturated Fat: 1g
- Cholesterol: 0mg
- Sodium: 700mg
- Total Carbohydrates: 50g
- Dietary Fiber: 14g
- Sugars: 10g
- Protein: 12g

Sink your teeth into a bowl of this Vampire Vegetarian Chili and enjoy a spooktacular meal that's perfect for mystery-solving appetites!

16. Goblin Granola Bars

Step into the mysterious world of Scooby-Doo with these Goblin Granola Bars that are sure to satisfy your hunger on any spooky adventure. Inspired by the snacks enjoyed by Scooby and the gang, these granola bars are a perfect combination of crunch and sweetness. Packed with wholesome ingredients, they're not only delicious but also provide the energy you need to unmask the mystery. Get ready to embark on a culinary journey that captures the essence of Scooby-Doo's gastronomic delights!

Serving: 12 bars
Preparation Time: 15 minutes
Ready Time: 2 hours (includes chilling time)

Ingredients:
- 2 cups old-fashioned rolled oats
- 1 cup crispy rice cereal
- 1/2 cup chopped nuts (e.g., almonds, walnuts)
- 1/2 cup dried fruits (e.g., raisins, cranberries)
- 1/4 cup shredded coconut
- 1/2 cup honey
- 1/4 cup unsalted butter
- 1/3 cup brown sugar, packed
- 1 teaspoon vanilla extract
- 1/2 teaspoon ground cinnamon
- 1/4 teaspoon salt
- 1/2 cup mini chocolate chips (optional, for an extra treat)

Instructions:
1. In a large bowl, combine the rolled oats, crispy rice cereal, chopped nuts, dried fruits, and shredded coconut. Set aside.
2. In a saucepan over medium heat, melt the butter and brown sugar together, stirring until the sugar has dissolved.
3. Add the honey, vanilla extract, ground cinnamon, and salt to the saucepan. Stir the mixture well and let it simmer for 2-3 minutes until it becomes a smooth, caramel-like sauce.
4. Pour the caramel sauce over the dry ingredients in the large bowl. Mix thoroughly until all the dry ingredients are coated evenly.
5. Line a baking dish with parchment paper, leaving some overhang on the sides for easy removal. Transfer the granola mixture to the dish and press it down firmly to create an even layer.
6. If desired, sprinkle mini chocolate chips over the top and press them into the granola.
7. Place the dish in the refrigerator and chill for at least 2 hours or until the granola bars are firm.
8. Once chilled, lift the parchment paper to easily remove the granola from the dish. Cut into bars of your preferred size.
9. Enjoy your Goblin Granola Bars on your next Scooby-Doo marathon or outdoor adventure!

Nutrition Information (per serving):
Calories: 220
Total Fat: 9g
Saturated Fat: 4g
Cholesterol: 10mg
Sodium: 55mg
Total Carbohydrates: 32g
Dietary Fiber: 3g
Sugars: 17g
Protein: 4g
Note: Nutrition information is approximate and may vary based on specific ingredients used.

17. Ghoulish Green Smoothie

Get ready to embark on a spooky culinary adventure with our "Ghoulish Green Smoothie," inspired by the mystery-solving antics of Scooby-Doo and the gang! This eerily delicious smoothie is not only a treat for the taste buds but also packs a nutritional punch. Packed with vibrant green hues and a mysterious blend of ingredients, this concoction is sure to satisfy your cravings for both flavor and fun. Whip it up for a ghoulishly good time at your next Scooby-Doo-themed gathering!

Serving: Makes 2 servings
Preparation Time: 15 minutes
Ready Time: 15 minutes

Ingredients:
- 2 cups fresh spinach leaves
- 1 cup green grapes, frozen
- 1 ripe banana
- 1/2 avocado, peeled and pitted
- 1/2 cup cucumber, peeled and chopped
- 1/2 cup pineapple chunks, frozen
- 1 cup coconut water
- 1 tablespoon chia seeds
- Ice cubes (optional, for a colder smoothie)

- Gummy worms (for garnish, optional)

Instructions:
1. Prepare the Ingredients: Wash the fresh spinach leaves, peel and chop the cucumber, peel and pit the avocado, and peel the banana.
2. Blend the Greens: In a blender, combine the fresh spinach leaves, frozen green grapes, banana, avocado, cucumber, and pineapple chunks.
3. Add Liquid: Pour in the coconut water to help blend the ingredients smoothly. If you prefer a thicker consistency, you can adjust the amount of coconut water to your liking.
4. Boost with Chia Seeds: Add chia seeds to the blender for an extra nutritional boost. Chia seeds also add a fun texture to the smoothie.
5. Blend Until Smooth: Blend all the ingredients until you achieve a smooth and creamy texture. If desired, add ice cubes and blend again for a colder smoothie.
6. Serve: Pour the Ghoulish Green Smoothie into glasses. For an extra spooky touch, garnish with gummy worms.
7. Enjoy: Sip on this mysterious green delight and let the flavors transport you to a Scooby-Doo-worthy adventure!

Nutrition Information:
(Per Serving)
- Calories: 180
- Protein: 4g
- Fat: 8g
- Carbohydrates: 28g
- Fiber: 8g
- Sugar: 14g
- Vitamin C: 45mg
- Iron: 2mg
- Calcium: 120mg

Note: Nutrition information is approximate and may vary based on specific ingredients used.

18. Phantom Popcorn

Step into the mysterious world of Scooby-Doo with this delightful treat that captures the essence of intrigue and excitement – Phantom Popcorn!

Inspired by the numerous ghostly encounters and mysteries solved by the Scooby-Doo gang, this popcorn is sure to add a playful and flavorful twist to your snacking experience. Get ready to embark on a flavor adventure that combines the thrill of solving mysteries with the classic comfort of popcorn.

Serving: 4 servings
Preparation Time: 10 minutes
Ready Time: 15 minutes

Ingredients:
- 1/2 cup popcorn kernels
- 3 tablespoons unsalted butter
- 1/4 cup sugar
- 1/4 cup light corn syrup
- 1/2 teaspoon vanilla extract
- 1/4 teaspoon baking soda
- 1/4 teaspoon salt
- Purple and black food coloring (gel or powder)

Instructions:
1. Pop the Popcorn:
- Pop the popcorn kernels using your preferred method, whether it's an air popper, stovetop, or microwave.
2. Prepare the Syrup:
- In a saucepan over medium heat, melt the butter. Stir in the sugar, light corn syrup, vanilla extract, baking soda, and salt. Cook, stirring constantly, until the mixture comes to a boil.
3. Color the Syrup:
- Divide the syrup mixture into two bowls. Add a few drops of purple food coloring to one bowl and black food coloring to the other. Stir each until the color is evenly distributed.
4. Coat the Popcorn:
- Place the popped popcorn in a large bowl. Drizzle the colored syrups over the popcorn and gently toss to coat evenly. Be cautious as the syrup will be hot.
5. Bake the Popcorn:
- Preheat the oven to 250°F (120°C). Spread the coated popcorn on a baking sheet lined with parchment paper. Bake for 10-12 minutes, stirring halfway through, until the syrup has set.

6. Cool and Break Apart:
- Allow the Phantom Popcorn to cool completely on the baking sheet. Once cooled, break the popcorn into clusters.

7. Serve and Enjoy:
- Scoop the Phantom Popcorn into bowls or individual servings and get ready to enjoy a delicious and mysterious snack that pays homage to Scooby-Doo!

Nutrition Information:
(Per Serving)
- Calories: 180
- Total Fat: 8g
- Saturated Fat: 5g
- Cholesterol: 20mg
- Sodium: 160mg
- Total Carbohydrates: 27g
- Dietary Fiber: 2g
- Sugars: 15g
- Protein: 1g

Note: Nutrition information is approximate and may vary based on specific ingredients and serving sizes.

19. Swampy S'mores

Step into the mysterious world of Scooby-Doo with a delightful treat that captures the essence of adventures in the spooky swamps – Swampy S'mores! Inspired by the gang's escapades in creepy locales, these gooey delights are a perfect combination of the classic campfire treat and the eerie atmosphere of Scooby-Doo. Get ready to embark on a flavor journey that's both comforting and a little bit spooky.

Serving: Makes 8 servings.
Preparation Time: 15 minutes
Ready Time: 30 minutes

Ingredients:
- 16 whole graham crackers
- 8 marshmallows

- 200g milk chocolate, chopped
- 1 cup mini marshmallows
- 1/2 cup crushed chocolate sandwich cookies (for the "swamp" texture)
- 1/4 cup unsalted butter
- 1/4 teaspoon salt

Instructions:
1. Preheat your oven to 350°F (175°C) and line a baking sheet with parchment paper.
2. Break the graham crackers in half, creating squares, and place them on the prepared baking sheet.
3. In a small saucepan over low heat, melt the butter. Add the chopped chocolate and stir until smooth.
4. Spread a thin layer of the melted chocolate on each graham cracker square.
5. Place a marshmallow in the center of half of the squares.
6. Sprinkle mini marshmallows and crushed chocolate sandwich cookies over the chocolate-covered graham crackers without marshmallows.
7. Carefully toast the marshmallow-topped graham crackers under a broiler for 1-2 minutes or until the marshmallows are golden brown.
8. Remove from the oven and place a marshmallow-topped graham cracker on top of a chocolate-covered, cookie-crusted one to create a sandwich.
9. Press gently to allow the marshmallow to ooze out, creating a swampy effect.
10. Allow the Swampy S'mores to cool for a few minutes before serving.

Nutrition Information:
(Per Serving)
- Calories: 320
- Total Fat: 16g
- Saturated Fat: 8g
- Trans Fat: 0g
- Cholesterol: 15mg
- Sodium: 200mg
- Total Carbohydrates: 42g
- Dietary Fiber: 2g
- Sugars: 24g
- Protein: 3g

Uncover the mystery and sweetness of the swamp with these Swampy S'mores – a perfect treat for Scooby-Doo fans of all ages!

20. Monster Meatball Sliders

Step into the world of mystery and mayhem with these "Monster Meatball Sliders," inspired by the iconic Scooby-Doo and the gang. These savory sliders are a delectable combination of juicy meatballs, gooey cheese, and zesty sauce, making them the perfect treat for your next Scooby-Doo-themed gathering. Get ready to unmask your appetite with these mouthwatering sliders that even the Mystery Inc. crew would love!

Serving: Makes approximately 12 sliders.
Preparation Time: 20 minutes
Ready Time: 40 minutes

Ingredients:
- 1 pound ground beef
- 1/2 cup breadcrumbs
- 1/4 cup grated Parmesan cheese
- 1/4 cup chopped fresh parsley
- 2 cloves garlic, minced
- 1 teaspoon dried oregano
- 1 teaspoon dried basil
- Salt and pepper to taste
- 1 cup marinara sauce
- 1 cup shredded mozzarella cheese
- 12 slider buns
- Butter for toasting buns
- Optional: sliced olives for "monster eyes"

Instructions:
1. Preheat your oven to 375°F (190°C).
2. In a large bowl, combine ground beef, breadcrumbs, Parmesan cheese, chopped parsley, minced garlic, oregano, basil, salt, and pepper. Mix until well combined.
3. Form the mixture into 12 meatballs, each about the size of a golf ball.

4. In a skillet over medium heat, brown the meatballs on all sides until cooked through, approximately 8-10 minutes.
5. While the meatballs are cooking, split the slider buns and lightly butter the cut sides. Toast the buns in the oven for a few minutes until golden brown.
6. Once the meatballs are cooked, place them on the bottom half of each slider bun.
7. Spoon marinara sauce over each meatball and sprinkle with shredded mozzarella cheese.
8. Optional: Create "monster eyes" by placing sliced olives on top of the cheese.
9. Place the sliders on a baking sheet and bake in the oven until the cheese is melted and bubbly, about 10 minutes.
10. Remove from the oven and place the top half of the slider buns on each. Serve warm and enjoy the monster-sized flavor!

Nutrition Information:
(Per Serving - 1 Slider)
- Calories: 280
- Total Fat: 15g
- Saturated Fat: 6g
- Cholesterol: 45mg
- Sodium: 480mg
- Total Carbohydrates: 21g
- Dietary Fiber: 2g
- Sugars: 3g
- Protein: 16g

Note: Nutrition information is approximate and may vary based on specific ingredients used.

21. Shiver Shake

Step into the world of mystery-solving with the "Shiver Shake," a chilling concoction inspired by the spine-tingling adventures of Scooby-Doo and the gang. This frosty treat is a delightful blend of flavors that will leave you shivering with delight. Perfect for cooling down after solving a puzzling case or just enjoying a spooky movie night.

Serving: 2 servings
Preparation Time: 10 minutes
Ready Time: 10 minutes

Ingredients:
- 2 cups vanilla ice cream
- 1 cup milk
- 1/2 cup chocolate syrup
- 1/4 cup peanut butter
- 1 teaspoon vanilla extract
- Whipped cream, for topping
- Chocolate shavings or crushed peanuts, for garnish (optional)

Instructions:
1. In a blender, combine the vanilla ice cream, milk, chocolate syrup, peanut butter, and vanilla extract.
2. Blend the ingredients until smooth and creamy, ensuring a well-mixed consistency.
3. Pour the Shiver Shake into two glasses.
4. Top each shake with a generous dollop of whipped cream.
5. For an extra touch of decadence, sprinkle chocolate shavings or crushed peanuts on top (optional).
6. Grab a straw and enjoy your chilling Shiver Shake!

Nutrition Information:
(Per Serving)
- Calories: 450
- Total Fat: 25g
- Saturated Fat: 12g
- Trans Fat: 0g
- Cholesterol: 45mg
- Sodium: 180mg
- Total Carbohydrates: 48g
- Dietary Fiber: 2g
- Sugars: 38g
- Protein: 10g
- Vitamin D: 2%
- Calcium: 30%
- Iron: 6%
- Potassium: 15%

Note: Nutrition information is approximate and may vary based on specific ingredients and serving sizes. Adjustments can be made based on dietary preferences or restrictions. Enjoy your Shiver Shake, and may it bring a hint of mystery and nostalgia to your taste buds!

22. Witches' Brew Punch

Step into the mysterious world of Scooby-Doo with this enchanting concoction, aptly named Witches' Brew Punch. Inspired by the spooky adventures of the Mystery Inc. gang, this bewitching beverage is perfect for gatherings, parties, or any occasion where a touch of the supernatural is in order. Packed with vibrant colors and tantalizing flavors, Witches' Brew Punch is sure to cast a spell on your taste buds.

Serving: This recipe serves 8-10 guests, making it an ideal choice for a spirited get-together.
Preparation Time: 15 minutes
Ready Time: 2 hours (includes chilling time)

Ingredients:
- 2 cups grape juice
- 2 cups orange juice
- 1 cup pineapple juice
- 1 cup ginger ale
- 1/2 cup lemonade
- 1/4 cup grenadine syrup
- 1 cup mixed berries (blueberries, raspberries, strawberries)
- 1 orange, sliced
- 1 lemon, sliced
- Ice cubes

Instructions:
1. In a large punch bowl, combine the grape juice, orange juice, pineapple juice, ginger ale, and lemonade.
2. Gently stir in the grenadine syrup to create a swirl effect.
3. Add the mixed berries, orange slices, and lemon slices to the punch bowl. Stir gently to combine.

4. Place the punch bowl in the refrigerator to chill for at least 2 hours, allowing the flavors to meld.
5. Just before serving, add ice cubes to the punch bowl for a refreshing touch.
6. Ladle the Witches' Brew Punch into individual glasses, making sure to include some fruit and berries in each serving.
7. Serve your bewitching brew to your guests and watch as they delight in the vibrant colors and delicious flavors.

Nutrition Information:
Note: Nutrition information is per serving (based on 8 servings)
- Calories: 120
- Total Fat: 0g
- Saturated Fat: 0g
- Cholesterol: 0mg
- Sodium: 10mg
- Total Carbohydrates: 30g
- Dietary Fiber: 2g
- Sugars: 24g
- Protein: 1g

Embrace the supernatural vibes of Scooby-Doo with Witches' Brew Punch—a delightful and visually stunning beverage that captures the essence of mystery and fun. Cheers to solving the mysteries of flavor!

23. Goblin Goulash

Get ready to embark on a culinary adventure with the mystery-solving gang and their lovable Great Dane, Scooby-Doo! In this cookbook, we bring you 103 food ideas inspired by the iconic moments and spooky locales encountered by Scooby and the gang. Our first recipe, "Goblin Goulash," pays homage to the many monsters and mysterious creatures the gang encounters on their thrilling journeys.

Serving: 4 servings
Preparation Time: 15 minutes
Ready Time: 1 hour

Ingredients:

- 1 pound beef stew meat, cubed
- 2 tablespoons vegetable oil
- 1 onion, finely chopped
- 2 cloves garlic, minced
- 1 bell pepper, diced
- 2 carrots, sliced
- 1 can (14 ounces) diced tomatoes
- 2 cups beef broth
- 1 cup red wine (optional)
- 1 teaspoon dried thyme
- 1 teaspoon dried rosemary
- 1 teaspoon paprika
- Salt and pepper to taste
- 1 cup frozen peas
- 2 tablespoons tomato paste
- 1 tablespoon Worcestershire sauce
- Cooked rice or mashed potatoes for serving

Instructions:
1. In a large pot or Dutch oven, heat the vegetable oil over medium-high heat. Add the beef stew meat and brown on all sides. Remove the meat from the pot and set it aside.
2. In the same pot, add the chopped onion, minced garlic, diced bell pepper, and sliced carrots. Sauté until the vegetables are softened.
3. Pour in the diced tomatoes, beef broth, and red wine (if using). Stir in the dried thyme, dried rosemary, paprika, salt, and pepper.
4. Return the browned beef to the pot. Stir in the frozen peas, tomato paste, and Worcestershire sauce.
5. Bring the goulash to a boil, then reduce the heat to low. Cover and simmer for about 45 minutes to 1 hour, or until the beef is tender and the flavors have melded together.
6. Serve the Goblin Goulash over cooked rice or mashed potatoes.

Nutrition Information:
(Per serving)
- Calories: 380
- Total Fat: 15g
- Saturated Fat: 4g
- Cholesterol: 70mg
- Sodium: 800mg

- Total Carbohydrates: 25g
- Dietary Fiber: 5g
- Sugars: 8g
- Protein: 30g

Goblin Goulash is a hearty and comforting dish that will warm you up on even the spookiest of nights. Enjoy this Scooby-Doo inspired recipe with friends and family as you unravel the mysteries of the kitchen!

24. Eerie Eyeball Cake Pops

Step into the spooky world of Scooby-Doo with these Eerie Eyeball Cake Pops! Perfect for a haunted celebration or a Scooby-Doo-themed party, these whimsical treats will have everyone's eyes on the prize. Simple to make and frighteningly delicious, these cake pops are sure to delight both kids and adults. Get ready to unmask the fun with this mysterious and tasty recipe straight from the Scooby Gang's kitchen!

Serving: Makes approximately 18-20 cake pops.
Preparation Time: 30 minutes
Ready Time: 2 hours (including chilling time)

Ingredients:
- 1 box of your favorite cake mix (plus required ingredients per the package instructions)
- 1 cup of frosting (cream cheese or vanilla work well)
- White candy melts
- Red gel food coloring
- Blue or green M&M candies (for irises)
- Black decorating gel or icing

Instructions:
1. Bake the Cake:
Follow the instructions on the cake mix box to prepare the cake batter. Bake the cake according to the package instructions. Allow it to cool completely.
2. Crumble the Cake:

In a large bowl, crumble the cooled cake into fine crumbs. Add the frosting and mix until well combined. The mixture should be moist enough to hold together when shaped into balls.

3. Shape the Cake Balls:

Roll the cake mixture into small, round balls, about the size of a golf ball. Place them on a parchment-lined baking sheet.

4. Melt the Candy Coating:

In a microwave-safe bowl, melt the white candy melts according to the package instructions. Stir until smooth.

5. Dip Cake Balls:

Dip the tip of a lollipop stick into the melted candy coating and insert it into a cake ball. This will help the cake pop stay on the stick. Dip each cake pop into the melted candy coating, ensuring it's fully covered. Allow any excess coating to drip off.

6. Create Eyeballs:

While the coating is still wet, place an M&M candy (color of your choice) in the center of the cake pop. Repeat this step for each cake pop. Allow the candy coating to set.

7. Add Details:

Use black decorating gel or icing to create the spooky veins and pupils on the eyeballs. Get creative and make each one unique!

8. Chill:

Place the cake pops in the refrigerator for at least 1 hour to allow the coating to fully set.

9. Serve:

Once set, arrange your Eerie Eyeball Cake Pops on a serving platter. Enjoy the mysterious and delicious treats with your fellow ghost hunters!

Nutrition Information:

(Note: Nutritional values are approximate and may vary based on specific ingredients and quantities used.)

- Calories per serving: Approximately 150
- Fat: 8g
- Carbohydrates: 20g
- Sugar: 15g
- Protein: 1g

25. Specter Spinach Dip

Step into the world of mystery and intrigue with the Specter Spinach Dip, inspired by the adventures of Scooby-Doo and the gang. This delectable dip is not only a treat for your taste buds but also a nod to the mysterious and exciting tales of the beloved Scooby-Doo series. Whip up this savory concoction for your next gathering and watch it disappear faster than Scooby and Shaggy can devour a box of Scooby Snacks!

Serving: Ideal for 6-8 hungry detectives.
Preparation Time: 15 minutes
Ready Time: 30 minutes

Ingredients:
- 1 ½ cups frozen chopped spinach, thawed and drained
- 1 cup mayonnaise
- 1 cup sour cream
- 1 cup grated Parmesan cheese
- 1 cup shredded mozzarella cheese
- 1 teaspoon minced garlic
- 1 teaspoon onion powder
- 1 teaspoon dried oregano
- 1 teaspoon dried basil
- ½ teaspoon salt
- ½ teaspoon black pepper
- 1 loaf of bread or tortilla chips for serving

Instructions:
1. Preheat your oven to 350°F (175°C).
2. In a large mixing bowl, combine the thawed and drained chopped spinach, mayonnaise, sour cream, Parmesan cheese, mozzarella cheese, minced garlic, onion powder, dried oregano, dried basil, salt, and black pepper. Mix until all ingredients are well combined.
3. Transfer the mixture into a baking dish, spreading it evenly.
4. Bake in the preheated oven for 20-25 minutes or until the dip is hot and bubbly, and the top is golden brown.
5. Remove from the oven and let it cool for a few minutes before serving.
6. Serve the Specter Spinach Dip with slices of bread or tortilla chips for dipping.

Nutrition Information:
Note: Nutritional values are approximate and may vary based on specific ingredients used.
- Calories per serving: 280
- Total Fat: 24g
- Saturated Fat: 8g
- Trans Fat: 0g
- Cholesterol: 35mg
- Sodium: 550mg
- Total Carbohydrates: 8g
- Dietary Fiber: 2g
- Sugars: 2g
- Protein: 8g

Uncover the mystery behind the irresistible flavors of the Specter Spinach Dip, a delightful addition to your Scooby-Doo-inspired culinary repertoire. Enjoy the magic and nostalgia as you savor every scoop of this delicious dip with friends and family!

26. Ghostly Guacamole

Step into the spooky world of Mystery Inc. with this hauntingly delicious "Ghostly Guacamole" inspired by Scooby-Doo! A ghoulish twist on the classic guacamole, this eerie green dip is perfect for Scooby-Doo enthusiasts and anyone looking to add a hint of mystery to their culinary adventures. It's a frightfully flavorful treat that's sure to have you saying, "Scooby-Dooby-Doo, where are you?"

Serving: This spooktacular Ghostly Guacamole serves 4-6 hungry detectives.
Preparation Time: 15 minutes
Ready Time: 15 minutes

Ingredients:
- 3 ripe avocados
- 1 lime, juiced
- 1/2 cup diced red onion
- 1 medium tomato, diced

- 1/4 cup chopped fresh cilantro
- 2 cloves garlic, minced
- 1 jalapeño, seeds and membranes removed, finely chopped
- Salt and pepper to taste
- Tortilla chips, for serving

Instructions:
1. Prepare the Avocados:
- Cut the avocados in half, remove the pits, and scoop the flesh into a bowl.
2. Mash the Avocados:
- Mash the avocados with a fork or potato masher until you achieve your desired level of creaminess.
3. Add Lime Juice:
- Squeeze the juice of one lime into the mashed avocados. This not only adds a zesty flavor but also helps prevent browning.
4. Mix in Vegetables:
- Gently fold in the diced red onion, tomato, cilantro, minced garlic, and chopped jalapeño.
5. Season to Taste:
- Season the guacamole with salt and pepper to taste. Adjust the seasonings according to your preference.
6. Chill and Serve:
- For optimal flavor, cover the guacamole with plastic wrap, pressing it directly against the surface to minimize browning. Chill in the refrigerator for at least 10 minutes before serving.
7. Serve with Tortilla Chips:
- Accompany your Ghostly Guacamole with a side of tortilla chips for a spine-tingling snack.

Nutrition Information:
(Per Serving)
- Calories: 180
- Total Fat: 15g
- Saturated Fat: 2g
- Trans Fat: 0g
- Cholesterol: 0mg
- Sodium: 10mg
- Total Carbohydrates: 12g
- Dietary Fiber: 8g

- Sugars: 2g
- Protein: 3g

Unmask the flavor mystery with this Ghostly Guacamole, a chillingly good addition to your Scooby-Doo-inspired culinary collection!

27. Bat Bites

Get ready for a mysterious and delicious adventure with these "Bat Bites" inspired by Scooby-Doo! These spooky snacks are perfect for any Scooby-Doo-themed gathering or just a fun snack for fans of the Mystery Inc. gang. Packed with flavor and a touch of mystery, these Bat Bites are sure to be a hit at your next snack time investigation!

Serving: Makes approximately 24 Bat Bites
Preparation Time: 15 minutes
Ready Time: 30 minutes

Ingredients:
- 1 package (17.3 ounces) puff pastry sheets, thawed
- 1 cup cooked and shredded chicken
- 1/2 cup cream cheese, softened
- 1/4 cup finely chopped red bell pepper
- 1/4 cup finely chopped green onion
- 1 teaspoon garlic powder
- 1 teaspoon onion powder
- 1/2 teaspoon dried oregano
- 1/2 teaspoon salt
- 1/4 teaspoon black pepper
- 1 large egg, beaten (for egg wash)

Instructions:
1. Preheat your oven to 400°F (200°C) and line a baking sheet with parchment paper.
2. In a mixing bowl, combine the shredded chicken, cream cheese, red bell pepper, green onion, garlic powder, onion powder, dried oregano, salt, and black pepper. Mix until well combined.
3. Roll out the puff pastry sheets on a lightly floured surface. Using a bat-shaped cookie cutter, cut out bat shapes from the puff pastry sheets.

4. Place a spoonful of the chicken mixture in the center of half of the bat shapes. Place the remaining bat shapes on top, creating a sandwich. Use a fork to press down and seal the edges.
5. Brush the tops of the bat bites with the beaten egg for a golden finish.
6. Transfer the bat bites to the prepared baking sheet and bake in the preheated oven for 15-20 minutes or until the pastry is golden brown and puffed up.
7. Allow the Bat Bites to cool slightly before serving. Serve with your favorite dipping sauce for an extra tasty experience!

Nutrition Information:
(Per serving - 2 Bat Bites)
- Calories: 180
- Total Fat: 12g
- Saturated Fat: 5g
- Trans Fat: 0g
- Cholesterol: 30mg
- Sodium: 250mg
- Total Carbohydrates: 14g
- Dietary Fiber: 1g
- Sugars: 1g
- Protein: 5g

Get ready to unmask the flavor in every bite of these Bat Bites – a snack that will have everyone saying, "Scooby-Dooby-Doo, where are you?" Enjoy!

28. Enchanted Edamame

Step into the world of mystery and adventure with the "Enchanted Edamame" recipe inspired by Scooby-Doo and his gang's escapades. These delightful seasoned edamame beans are sure to be a hit at your next gathering, whether you're solving mysteries or just enjoying a snack. Get ready to embark on a flavor-filled journey with this simple yet enchanting recipe!

Serving: 4 servings
Preparation Time: 10 minutes
Ready Time: 15 minutes

Ingredients:
- 2 cups frozen edamame, in their pods
- 1 tablespoon olive oil
- 2 cloves garlic, minced
- 1 teaspoon smoked paprika
- 1/2 teaspoon cumin
- 1/2 teaspoon onion powder
- 1/4 teaspoon cayenne pepper (adjust to taste)
- Salt and pepper to taste
- 1 tablespoon sesame seeds (optional, for garnish)
- Fresh cilantro or parsley for garnish

Instructions:
1. Prepare the Edamame:
- Thaw the frozen edamame according to package instructions if necessary.
- Steam or boil the edamame pods for 5-7 minutes, until they are tender but still have a slight crunch. Drain and set aside.
2. Seasoning Mixture:
- In a pan, heat the olive oil over medium heat. Add minced garlic and sauté until fragrant.
- Stir in smoked paprika, cumin, onion powder, and cayenne pepper. Cook for an additional 1-2 minutes, allowing the spices to release their flavors.
3. Coat the Edamame:
- Add the steamed edamame to the pan, tossing them to coat evenly with the seasoned oil. Cook for an additional 2-3 minutes, allowing the flavors to meld.
4. Adjust Seasoning:
- Season with salt and pepper to taste. Adjust cayenne pepper if you desire more heat.
5. Garnish and Serve:
- Transfer the enchanted edamame to a serving dish. Sprinkle sesame seeds and fresh cilantro or parsley on top for a finishing touch.

Nutrition Information:
- *Note: Nutritional values may vary based on specific ingredients and quantities used.*
- Calories: 120 per serving

- Protein: 8g
- Fat: 7g
- Carbohydrates: 10g
- Fiber: 4g
- Sugar: 2g
- Sodium: 200mg

Unleash the magic of Scooby-Doo with this Enchanted Edamame recipe, perfect for snacking during your next mystery-solving marathon or gathering with friends. Enjoy the delightful combination of flavors inspired by the beloved characters and their timeless adventures!

29. Jack-O'-Lantern Jello

Step into the spooky world of Scooby-Doo with this delightful Jack-O'-Lantern Jello, a treat that captures the essence of mystery and fun. Perfect for Halloween or any Scooby-Doo-themed gathering, this wiggly, giggly dessert is sure to bring smiles and excitement to your table. Follow the simple steps below to create a festive and flavorful experience that even Scooby and the gang would approve of!

Serving: Serves 8
Preparation Time: 20 minutes
Ready Time: 4 hours (includes chilling time)

Ingredients:
- 2 (3-ounce) packages orange-flavored gelatin
- 1 cup boiling water
- 1 cup cold water
- 1/2 cup orange juice
- 1/4 cup lemon juice
- 1 tablespoon sugar
- 1/2 teaspoon vanilla extract
- 8 small plastic or silicone Jack-O'-Lantern molds
- Cooking spray

Instructions:
1. In a heatproof bowl, combine the orange-flavored gelatin with 1 cup of boiling water. Stir well until the gelatin is completely dissolved.

2. Add 1 cup of cold water to the gelatin mixture, followed by the orange juice and lemon juice. Mix thoroughly.
3. Stir in the sugar and vanilla extract until the sugar is dissolved.
4. Lightly coat the Jack-O'-Lantern molds with cooking spray to help with easy removal later.
5. Carefully pour the gelatin mixture into the prepared molds, filling them to the top.
6. Place the molds in the refrigerator and allow the Jello to set for at least 4 hours or until firm.
7. Once the Jello is set, gently remove the Jack-O'-Lanterns from the molds by running a knife around the edges and inverting them onto a serving plate.
8. Optional: For an extra spooky touch, add whipped cream or candy eyes on top of the Jack-O'-Lanterns.
9. Serve and enjoy the wiggly, jiggly fun of your Scooby-Doo-inspired Jack-O'-Lantern Jello!

Nutrition Information:
Note: Nutritional values may vary based on specific ingredients and brands used.
- Calories per serving: 80
- Total Fat: 0g
- Cholesterol: 0mg
- Sodium: 45mg
- Total Carbohydrates: 18g
- Sugars: 16g
- Protein: 2g

Capture the mystery and sweetness of Scooby-Doo with this Jack-O'-Lantern Jello—a treat that's as fun to make as it is to eat!

30. Devilish Deviled Eggs

Get ready to embark on a culinary adventure with Scooby-Doo and the gang! Our "Devilish Deviled Eggs" recipe is a spooky twist on a classic favorite, perfect for any Scooby-Doo-themed gathering. These eggs are devilishly delicious, and the mystery lies in the zesty flavors that will leave your taste buds tingling. So, gather your Scooby snacks and let's dive into this hauntingly good recipe!

Serving: Makes 24 deviled eggs
Preparation Time: 15 minutes
Ready Time: 30 minutes

Ingredients:
- 12 hard-boiled eggs, peeled and cut in half lengthwise
- 1/3 cup mayonnaise
- 2 teaspoons Dijon mustard
- 1 teaspoon white vinegar
- 1/2 teaspoon salt
- 1/4 teaspoon black pepper
- 1/4 teaspoon garlic powder
- 1/4 teaspoon smoked paprika (plus extra for garnish)
- Chives or green onions, finely chopped (for garnish)

Instructions:
1. Carefully remove the yolks from the halved eggs and place them in a bowl.
2. Mash the egg yolks with a fork and add mayonnaise, Dijon mustard, white vinegar, salt, black pepper, garlic powder, and smoked paprika. Mix until well combined and smooth.
3. Spoon or pipe the yolk mixture back into the egg whites, creating a devilish appearance.
4. Sprinkle additional smoked paprika on top for an extra smoky kick.
5. Garnish each deviled egg with chopped chives or green onions to add a pop of color and freshness.
6. Chill in the refrigerator for at least 15 minutes before serving.

Nutrition Information:
Per serving (1 deviled egg):
- Calories: 70
- Total Fat: 6g
- Saturated Fat: 1.5g
- Trans Fat: 0g
- Cholesterol: 190mg
- Sodium: 130mg
- Total Carbohydrates: 0.5g
- Dietary Fiber: 0g
- Sugars: 0g

- Protein: 3g

Enjoy these Devilish Deviled Eggs at your next Scooby-Doo-themed party, and watch them disappear mysteriously!

31. Zombie Zone Nachos

Step into the mysterious and adventurous world of Scooby-Doo with our "Zombie Zone Nachos" — a spine-chilling snack that's perfect for your next Scooby-Doo marathon or themed party. These nachos are inspired by the many spooky encounters our favorite detective team has faced in haunted locations. Packed with bold flavors and a touch of mystery, these nachos are sure to satisfy your cravings while keeping you on the edge of your seat.

Serving: Serves 4
Preparation Time: 15 minutes
Ready Time: 20 minutes

Ingredients:
- 1 bag (10 oz) tortilla chips
- 1 cup shredded cooked chicken
- 1 cup shredded cheddar cheese
- 1 cup black beans, drained and rinsed
- 1 cup diced tomatoes
- 1/2 cup sliced black olives
- 1/2 cup sliced jalapeños (optional for extra kick)
- 1/2 cup diced red onions
- 1/2 cup sour cream
- 1/4 cup chopped fresh cilantro
- 1/4 cup sliced green onions
- 1 teaspoon ground cumin
- 1 teaspoon chili powder
- Salt and pepper to taste

Instructions:
1. Preheat your oven to 350°F (175°C).
2. On a large oven-safe platter or baking sheet, spread out the tortilla chips in an even layer.

3. In a small bowl, mix the shredded chicken with cumin, chili powder, salt, and pepper. Evenly distribute the seasoned chicken over the tortilla chips.
4. Sprinkle shredded cheddar cheese over the chips and chicken, ensuring good coverage.
5. Scatter black beans, diced tomatoes, black olives, and jalapeños (if using) over the nachos.
6. Place the platter or baking sheet in the preheated oven and bake for about 10 minutes or until the cheese is melted and bubbly.
7. Remove from the oven and top with diced red onions, dollops of sour cream, fresh cilantro, and sliced green onions.
8. Serve immediately while the nachos are hot and gooey. Enjoy the Scooby-Doo-inspired goodness!

Nutrition Information:
(Per serving)
- Calories: 450
- Total Fat: 22g
- Saturated Fat: 9g
- Trans Fat: 0g
- Cholesterol: 60mg
- Sodium: 680mg
- Total Carbohydrates: 42g
- Dietary Fiber: 7g
- Sugars: 2g
- Protein: 20g

Note: Nutrition information is approximate and may vary based on specific ingredients used. Adjust quantities according to personal dietary preferences.

32. Mysterious Meringue Cookies

Embark on a culinary adventure with our "Mysterious Meringue Cookies," inspired by the beloved Scooby-Doo and his gang's mysterious escapades. These ethereal treats will transport you to the world of mysteries and sweet delights, making them the perfect addition to your Scooby-Doo-inspired cookbook. Get ready to unmask the deliciousness!

Serving: Makes approximately 24 cookies
Preparation Time: 15 minutes
Ready Time: 2 hours (including baking and cooling)

Ingredients:
- 3 large egg whites, at room temperature
- 3/4 cup granulated sugar
- 1/4 teaspoon cream of tartar
- 1 teaspoon vanilla extract
- Pinch of salt
- Gel food coloring (optional)
- Edible googly eyes (optional)

Instructions:
1. Preheat the Oven: Preheat your oven to 225°F (110°C). Line two baking sheets with parchment paper.
2. Whip the Egg Whites: In a clean, dry bowl, whip the egg whites with an electric mixer until foamy. Add cream of tartar and continue whipping until soft peaks form.
3. Gradually Add Sugar: Gradually add the sugar, one tablespoon at a time, while continuing to whip the egg whites. Whip until glossy and stiff peaks form. This may take about 7-10 minutes.
4. Add Vanilla and Salt: Gently fold in the vanilla extract and a pinch of salt, ensuring not to deflate the meringue.
5. Pipe the Cookies: If desired, add a few drops of gel food coloring to achieve a mysterious, vibrant look. Transfer the meringue mixture to a piping bag fitted with a star tip. Pipe small mounds onto the prepared baking sheets.
6. Bake: Bake the meringue cookies in the preheated oven for 1.5 to 2 hours, or until they are dry and crisp. Rotate the sheets halfway through the baking time.
7. Cool Completely: Allow the cookies to cool completely on the baking sheets. If you want to add a fun touch, attach edible googly eyes using a dab of leftover meringue.
8. Serve and Enjoy: Once cooled, serve these mysterious meringue cookies on a Scooby-Doo-themed platter and enjoy the sweet sensation of solving a culinary mystery!

Nutrition Information:
(Per serving - 1 cookie)

- Calories: 25
- Total Fat: 0g
- Cholesterol: 0mg
- Sodium: 10mg
- Total Carbohydrates: 6g
- Sugars: 6g
- Protein: 0g

These Mysterious Meringue Cookies are not only a delight for the taste buds but also a whimsical addition to any Scooby-Doo-themed gathering. Get ready for a taste adventure that's as mysterious as the gang's escapades!

33. Cursed Carrot Sticks

Get ready to embark on a culinary adventure with our spooky and delicious recipe inspired by Scooby-Doo! Introducing "Cursed Carrot Sticks," a bewitching twist on a classic snack that's perfect for Scooby and the gang. These carrot sticks are not only a healthy treat but also carry an air of mystery that will leave your taste buds craving for more. So, grab your favorite mystery-solving pals and let's dive into the kitchen to whip up these hauntingly good snacks!

Serving: 4-6 servings
Preparation Time: 15 minutes
Ready Time: 30 minutes

Ingredients:
- 1 pound fresh carrots, peeled and cut into thin sticks
- 2 tablespoons olive oil
- 1 teaspoon garlic powder
- 1 teaspoon onion powder
- 1/2 teaspoon smoked paprika
- 1/2 teaspoon cumin
- 1/2 teaspoon salt
- 1/4 teaspoon black pepper
- 1/4 teaspoon cayenne pepper (adjust to taste for desired spiciness)
- 1 tablespoon honey
- 2 tablespoons chopped fresh parsley (for garnish)

Instructions:
1. Preheat your oven to 425°F (220°C).
2. In a large bowl, toss the carrot sticks with olive oil, garlic powder, onion powder, smoked paprika, cumin, salt, black pepper, and cayenne pepper until evenly coated.
3. Spread the seasoned carrot sticks in a single layer on a baking sheet.
4. Roast in the preheated oven for 20-25 minutes or until the carrots are tender and slightly caramelized, stirring once halfway through the cooking time.
5. Remove the carrot sticks from the oven and drizzle honey over them while they are still warm, tossing gently to coat.
6. Transfer the cursed carrot sticks to a serving platter, sprinkle with chopped fresh parsley, and serve immediately.

Nutrition Information:
Note: Nutritional values are approximate and may vary based on specific ingredients used.
- Calories per serving: 120
- Total Fat: 7g
- Saturated Fat: 1g
- Trans Fat: 0g
- Cholesterol: 0mg
- Sodium: 340mg
- Total Carbohydrates: 15g
- Dietary Fiber: 4g
- Sugars: 8g
- Protein: 1g

Unravel the mystery of flavor with these Cursed Carrot Sticks—a snack that's sure to vanish from the plate in no time! Enjoy these treats as you embark on your own culinary mysteries, just like Scooby and the gang.

34. Pumpkin Patch Pudding

Step into the world of mystery and adventure with Scooby-Doo and the gang as we unveil the secret behind the delectable Pumpkin Patch Pudding. This spooky yet delicious treat is sure to satisfy your sweet tooth, making it a perfect addition to your Scooby-Doo-inspired culinary journey. Packed with the warm flavors of pumpkin and a hint of mystery, this dessert is bound to be a hit with kids and adults alike.

Serving: Makes 6 servings
Preparation Time: 15 minutes
Ready Time: 2 hours (includes chilling time)

Ingredients:
- 1 cup canned pumpkin puree
- 1/2 cup brown sugar
- 1 teaspoon pumpkin pie spice
- 1/2 teaspoon cinnamon
- 1/4 teaspoon nutmeg
- 1/4 teaspoon salt
- 2 cups whole milk
- 1/2 cup heavy cream
- 1/2 cup granulated sugar
- 1/4 cup cornstarch
- 4 large egg yolks
- 2 tablespoons unsalted butter
- 1 teaspoon vanilla extract
- Ginger snap cookies (for garnish)

Instructions:
1. In a medium saucepan, combine the pumpkin puree, brown sugar, pumpkin pie spice, cinnamon, nutmeg, and salt. Cook over medium heat, stirring constantly, for about 5 minutes until the mixture is well combined and fragrant.
2. In a separate bowl, whisk together the milk, heavy cream, granulated sugar, and cornstarch until smooth.
3. Slowly pour the milk mixture into the saucepan with the pumpkin mixture, whisking constantly to avoid lumps. Continue to cook over medium heat, stirring constantly, until the pudding thickens. This should take about 8-10 minutes.
4. In a separate bowl, lightly beat the egg yolks. Gradually whisk in about a cup of the hot pumpkin mixture to temper the eggs. Then, pour the egg mixture back into the saucepan, whisking constantly.
5. Continue cooking the pudding over medium heat until it reaches a pudding-like consistency. This should take an additional 3-4 minutes.

6. Remove the saucepan from heat and stir in the butter and vanilla extract until smooth.

7. Pour the pudding into individual serving dishes or a large bowl. Cover with plastic wrap, ensuring it touches the surface of the pudding to prevent a skin from forming.

8. Chill the pudding in the refrigerator for at least 2 hours, allowing it to set.

9. Before serving, crush ginger snap cookies and sprinkle them over the top for a crunchy, flavorful garnish.

Nutrition Information:
(Per Serving)
- Calories: 320
- Fat: 15g
- Saturated Fat: 8g
- Cholesterol: 165mg
- Sodium: 180mg
- Carbohydrates: 42g
- Fiber: 2g
- Sugars: 32g
- Protein: 6g

Uncover the mysteries of the Pumpkin Patch Pudding and let the delicious flavors transport you to the world of Scooby-Doo and his friends!

35. Haunted Hash Browns

Step into the spooky world of Scooby-Doo with our "Haunted Hash Browns" recipe! Inspired by the thrilling mysteries and supernatural adventures of the Mystery Inc. gang, these hash browns are sure to add a touch of excitement to your breakfast or brunch. Packed with flavorful ingredients, this dish is a delightful and eerie twist on the classic hash browns. Get ready to solve the mystery of an unforgettable meal!

Serving: 4 servings
Preparation Time: 15 minutes
Ready Time: 30 minutes

Ingredients:
- 4 cups shredded potatoes (frozen hash browns or freshly grated)
- 1/2 cup diced onions
- 1/2 cup diced bell peppers (assorted colors for a vibrant touch)
- 1 cup shredded cheddar cheese
- 1/4 cup chopped fresh parsley
- 2 cloves garlic, minced
- 1 teaspoon smoked paprika
- 1/2 teaspoon onion powder
- 1/2 teaspoon garlic powder
- Salt and pepper to taste
- 2 tablespoons vegetable oil
- Cooking spray for greasing

Instructions:
1. Preheat the Oven:
Preheat your oven to 400°F (200°C).
2. Prepare the Hash Browns:
If using frozen hash browns, let them thaw slightly. If using fresh potatoes, squeeze out any excess moisture. In a large bowl, combine the shredded potatoes, diced onions, diced bell peppers, shredded cheddar cheese, chopped parsley, minced garlic, smoked paprika, onion powder, garlic powder, salt, and pepper. Mix well to ensure all ingredients are evenly distributed.
3. Form Patties:
Divide the mixture into 4 equal portions and shape them into round patties.
4. Cook on the Stovetop:
Heat vegetable oil in a large oven-safe skillet over medium heat. Add the hash brown patties and cook for 3-4 minutes on each side or until they are golden brown.
5. Transfer to Oven:
If your skillet is oven-safe, transfer it to the preheated oven.
Alternatively, transfer the hash brown patties to a baking sheet. Bake for an additional 15-20 minutes or until the hash browns are crispy and cooked through.
6. Serve:
Once done, remove from the oven and let them cool for a few minutes. Serve the haunted hash browns with your favorite dipping sauce or alongside eggs for a complete breakfast experience.

Nutrition Information:
Note: Nutritional values are approximate and may vary based on specific ingredients used.
- Calories per serving: 250
- Total Fat: 14g
- Saturated Fat: 7g
- Trans Fat: 0g
- Cholesterol: 25mg
- Sodium: 350mg
- Total Carbohydrates: 25g
- Dietary Fiber: 3g
- Sugars: 2g
- Protein: 8g

Enjoy your Haunted Hash Browns and get ready for a taste adventure inspired by the iconic Scooby-Doo!

36. Poltergeist Peanut Butter Cups

Step into the world of mystery and nostalgia with these "Poltergeist Peanut Butter Cups," inspired by the classic cartoon series, Scooby-Doo. These delectable treats are a playful twist on the traditional peanut butter cups, adding a hint of spookiness that even Scooby and the gang would approve of. Perfect for Halloween parties or any time you crave a delightful blend of chocolate and peanut butter.

Serving: Makes approximately 24 Poltergeist Peanut Butter Cups.
Preparation Time: 20 minutes
Ready Time: 1 hour (including chilling time)

Ingredients:
- 2 cups semi-sweet chocolate chips
- 1 cup creamy peanut butter
- 1/4 cup unsalted butter, softened
- 1 cup powdered sugar
- 1 teaspoon vanilla extract
- 1/2 teaspoon salt
- 1/4 cup graham cracker crumbs

- Optional: Ghost-shaped cookie cutter or silicone mold

Instructions:
1. In a microwave-safe bowl, melt 1 cup of chocolate chips in 30-second intervals, stirring after each, until fully melted. This will be the base layer for your peanut butter cups.
2. Using a spoon or a silicone brush, coat the bottom and sides of cupcake liners with the melted chocolate, creating a thin layer. Place the lined cupcake tin in the refrigerator to set.
3. In a separate bowl, mix together creamy peanut butter, softened butter, powdered sugar, vanilla extract, and salt until well combined. Fold in graham cracker crumbs to add a delightful crunch reminiscent of Scooby's favorite snacks.
4. Remove the cupcake tin from the refrigerator and evenly distribute the peanut butter mixture into each chocolate-coated cup, pressing it down gently.
5. Melt the remaining 1 cup of chocolate chips using the same method as before. Spoon the melted chocolate over the peanut butter layer, covering it completely.
6. If desired, use a ghost-shaped cookie cutter or silicone mold to create ghostly shapes with the remaining melted chocolate. Place these on top of each peanut butter cup.
7. Return the cupcake tin to the refrigerator and let it chill for at least 1 hour, allowing the peanut butter cups to set.
8. Once fully chilled and set, carefully remove the Poltergeist Peanut Butter Cups from the cupcake liners. Serve and enjoy the mysterious and delightful flavor!

Nutrition Information:
Note: Nutritional values are approximate and may vary based on specific ingredients used.
- Serving Size: 1 Poltergeist Peanut Butter Cup
- Calories: 150
- Total Fat: 10g
- Saturated Fat: 4g
- Cholesterol: 5mg
- Sodium: 70mg
- Total Carbohydrates: 15g
- Dietary Fiber: 1g
- Sugars: 11g

- Protein: 3g

Embrace the spooky fun of Scooby-Doo with these Poltergeist Peanut Butter Cups that are sure to satisfy your sweet tooth and transport you back to the adventures of Mystery Inc.

37. Abominable Apple Pie

Embark on a culinary adventure with the mysterious and mouthwatering "Abominable Apple Pie," inspired by the classic animated series, Scooby-Doo. This delightful dessert pays homage to the thrilling escapades of Mystery Inc., combining the warmth of homemade apple pie with a playful twist that's sure to keep you guessing.

Serving: 8 servings
Preparation Time: 20 minutes
Ready Time: 1 hour and 30 minutes

Ingredients:
- 6 cups peeled, cored, and sliced apples (a mix of Granny Smith and Honeycrisp works well)
- 1 tablespoon lemon juice
- 1/2 cup granulated sugar
- 1/2 cup light brown sugar, packed
- 1 teaspoon ground cinnamon
- 1/4 teaspoon ground nutmeg
- 1/4 teaspoon salt
- 2 tablespoons all-purpose flour
- 1 package refrigerated pie crusts (or homemade if you prefer)
- 1 egg, beaten (for egg wash)

Instructions:
1. Preheat your oven to 375°F (190°C).
2. In a large bowl, combine the sliced apples and lemon juice, tossing to coat the apples and prevent browning.
3. In a separate bowl, mix together the granulated sugar, brown sugar, cinnamon, nutmeg, salt, and flour.
4. Add the sugar mixture to the apples, tossing until the apples are evenly coated.

5. Roll out one pie crust and place it into a 9-inch pie dish, allowing the edges to hang over.
6. Pour the apple mixture into the crust, spreading it evenly.
7. Roll out the second pie crust and place it on top of the apple filling. Trim and crimp the edges to seal the pie.
8. Make several small slits on the top crust to allow steam to escape.
9. Brush the top crust with the beaten egg, creating a golden finish when baked.
10. Place the pie on a baking sheet to catch any drips and bake for 50-60 minutes, or until the crust is golden brown, and the filling is bubbly.
11. Allow the pie to cool for at least 30 minutes before serving.

Nutrition Information:
(Per serving)
- Calories: 320
- Total Fat: 12g
- Saturated Fat: 4g
- Cholesterol: 20mg
- Sodium: 280mg
- Total Carbohydrates: 52g
- Dietary Fiber: 4g
- Sugars: 30g
- Protein: 3g

Indulge in the mystery and flavor of the Abominable Apple Pie – a delectable treat that even Scooby-Doo would find irresistible!

38. Batty Banana Bread

Unearth the mysterious and delightful flavors of Scooby-Doo with our "Batty Banana Bread" recipe. Inspired by the quirky and adventurous spirit of the beloved Scooby-Doo series, this banana bread is a perfect blend of sweetness and spookiness. Whether you're solving mysteries with the Mystery Inc. gang or just enjoying a snack, this treat is sure to satisfy your taste buds.

Serving: Makes one loaf (about 10 slices)
Preparation Time: 15 minutes
Ready Time: 1 hour and 15 minutes

Ingredients:
- 3 ripe bananas, mashed
- 1/2 cup unsalted butter, melted
- 1 teaspoon vanilla extract
- 1 teaspoon baking soda
- A pinch of salt
- 1/2 cup granulated sugar
- 1/2 cup packed brown sugar
- 1 1/2 cups all-purpose flour
- 1/2 cup crushed bat-shaped chocolate cookies (for a spooky touch!)
- Optional: 1/2 cup chopped nuts (walnuts or pecans)

Instructions:
1. Preheat your oven to 350°F (175°C). Grease a 9x5-inch loaf pan.
2. In a large mixing bowl, mash the ripe bananas with a fork until smooth.
3. Stir the melted butter into the mashed bananas.
4. Add the vanilla extract, baking soda, and a pinch of salt to the banana mixture. Mix well.
5. Incorporate the granulated sugar and brown sugar into the banana mixture, stirring until smooth.
6. Gradually add the flour to the wet ingredients, mixing until just combined. Be careful not to overmix.
7. Fold in the crushed bat-shaped chocolate cookies and chopped nuts (if using).
8. Pour the batter into the prepared loaf pan, spreading it evenly.
9. Bake in the preheated oven for approximately 60-70 minutes or until a toothpick inserted into the center comes out clean.
10. Allow the banana bread to cool in the pan for 10 minutes before transferring it to a wire rack to cool completely.

Nutrition Information:
Per Serving (1 slice):
- Calories: 250
- Total Fat: 10g
- Saturated Fat: 6g
- Cholesterol: 25mg
- Sodium: 180mg
- Total Carbohydrates: 38g

- Dietary Fiber: 2g
- Sugars: 22g
- Protein: 3g

Indulge in the "Batty Banana Bread" and embark on a flavor adventure inspired by the wacky world of Scooby-Doo!

39. Mummy Mocha Latte

Unravel the mysteries of flavor with our bewitching beverage, the "Mummy Mocha Latte." Inspired by the suspenseful adventures of Scooby-Doo and the gang, this indulgent coffee creation is sure to tantalize your taste buds. Whether you're solving mysteries or just in need of a delicious pick-me-up, this Mocha Latte is the perfect companion.

Serving: 2 servings
Preparation Time: 10 minutes
Ready Time: 15 minutes

Ingredients:
- 2 cups strong brewed coffee
- 1 cup whole milk
- 1/4 cup cocoa powder
- 1/4 cup granulated sugar
- 1/4 cup dark chocolate chips
- 1 teaspoon vanilla extract
- Whipped cream, for topping
- Crushed chocolate cookies, for garnish

Instructions:
1. In a saucepan, combine the whole milk, cocoa powder, and sugar. Heat over medium-low heat, stirring constantly, until the mixture is well combined and heated through.
2. Add the dark chocolate chips to the milk mixture and continue to stir until the chocolate chips are completely melted.
3. Brew a strong cup of coffee. Pour the brewed coffee into the chocolate milk mixture and stir well.

4. Add the vanilla extract and continue to stir until the Mocha Latte is well combined.
5. Pour the Mummy Mocha Latte into mugs, leaving room at the top for toppings.
6. Top each mug with a generous dollop of whipped cream and sprinkle crushed chocolate cookies on top for a graveyard-inspired garnish.
7. Serve immediately and enjoy the hauntingly delicious Mummy Mocha Latte!

Nutrition Information:
Note: Nutritional values are approximate and may vary based on specific ingredients used.
- Calories per serving: 200
- Total Fat: 8g
- Saturated Fat: 5g
- Cholesterol: 12mg
- Sodium: 45mg
- Total Carbohydrates: 30g
- Dietary Fiber: 2g
- Sugars: 24g
- Protein: 4g

Unearth the rich flavors of this Mummy Mocha Latte, a spooktacular treat that will leave you craving more mystery and more coffee!

40. Wacky Witch Fingers (Cheese Sticks)

Get ready to embark on a spooky culinary adventure inspired by Scooby-Doo with these whimsically creepy Wacky Witch Fingers, a.k.a. Cheese Sticks! These eerie delights are perfect for a Scooby-Doo-themed gathering, Halloween party, or any time you want to add a touch of mystery to your snacks. Watch as your guests munch on these cheesy delights, wondering if they're under a spell or just enjoying a tasty treat!

Serving: Makes approximately 20 witch fingers.
Preparation Time: 15 minutes
Ready Time: 25 minutes

Ingredients:

- 1 package (8 ounces) refrigerated crescent roll dough
- 10 string cheese sticks, halved
- 20 almond slices
- 1 tablespoon unsalted butter, melted
- 1/2 teaspoon garlic powder
- 1/2 teaspoon dried oregano
- Marinara sauce for dipping (optional)

Instructions:
1. Preheat the Oven:
Preheat your oven to 375°F (190°C). Line a baking sheet with parchment paper.
2. Prepare the Dough:
Unroll the crescent roll dough and separate it into triangles. If needed, press the seams together to create a solid dough surface.
3. Cut the Cheese:
Cut each string cheese stick in half, creating 20 shorter sticks.
4. Wrap the Witches' Fingers:
Take one triangle of dough and place a halved cheese stick on the wider end. Roll the dough around the cheese stick, leaving a small section exposed to resemble a fingertip. Use a knife to make knuckle marks and press an almond slice at the tip to create a spooky nail. Repeat for all fingers.
5. Bake to Perfection:
Place the wrapped cheese fingers on the prepared baking sheet. In a small bowl, mix the melted butter, garlic powder, and dried oregano. Brush this mixture over the witch fingers for added flavor. Bake in the preheated oven for 10-12 minutes or until the dough turns golden brown.
6. Serve with a Side of Mystery:
Allow the witch fingers to cool for a few minutes before serving. For an extra mysterious touch, pair them with marinara sauce for dipping.

Nutrition Information:
(Per serving - 2 witch fingers)
- Calories: 180
- Total Fat: 10g
- Saturated Fat: 5g
- Cholesterol: 20mg
- Sodium: 380mg

- Total Carbohydrates: 14g
- Dietary Fiber: 0g
- Sugars: 3g
- Protein: 8g

These Wacky Witch Fingers are sure to cast a spell on your taste buds and add a dash of excitement to your Scooby-Doo-themed culinary experience! Enjoy the mystery and deliciousness that unfolds with every bite.

41. Goblin Grapes

Step into the mystical world of Scooby-Doo with our enchanting recipe for Goblin Grapes! These spooky yet delicious treats are perfect for any Scooby-Doo-themed gathering or a fun snack while watching your favorite mystery-solving team in action. The vibrant green hue and tantalizing flavor make Goblin Grapes an irresistible addition to your Scooby-Doo-inspired culinary adventure.

Serving: Makes approximately 20 Goblin Grapes
Preparation Time: 15 minutes
Ready Time: 1 hour (including chilling time)

Ingredients:
- 1 bunch green grapes
- 1 cup white chocolate chips
- 1 tablespoon coconut oil
- Green food coloring
- Black edible glitter (optional, for a magical touch)

Instructions:
1. Wash and Dry Grapes: Rinse the green grapes thoroughly under cold water and pat them dry with a paper towel. Make sure they are completely dry before proceeding.
2. Melt White Chocolate: In a microwave-safe bowl, combine the white chocolate chips and coconut oil. Microwave in 30-second intervals, stirring between each interval, until the chocolate is fully melted and smooth.

3. Add Food Coloring: Stir in a few drops of green food coloring into the melted white chocolate until you achieve the desired goblin green color.
4. Dip Grapes: Holding each grape by the stem, dip it into the green chocolate mixture, coating it evenly. Allow any excess chocolate to drip off.
5. Set on Parchment Paper: Place the chocolate-coated grapes on a parchment paper-lined tray. If using black edible glitter, sprinkle it over the grapes for a touch of magic.
6. Chill: Place the tray in the refrigerator for at least 1 hour or until the chocolate coating is firm.
7. Serve: Once the chocolate is set, remove the Goblin Grapes from the refrigerator. Arrange them on a platter and serve them at your Scooby-Doo-themed gathering.

Nutrition Information:
(Per Serving - 4 Goblin Grapes)
- Calories: 120
- Total Fat: 7g
- Saturated Fat: 5g
- Trans Fat: 0g
- Cholesterol: 2mg
- Sodium: 12mg
- Total Carbohydrates: 14g
- Dietary Fiber: 1g
- Sugars: 12g
- Protein: 1g

Enjoy these Goblin Grapes as a mystical and tasty addition to your Scooby-Doo culinary experience!

42. Phantom Pita Chips

Transport yourself to the spooky world of Scooby-Doo with these tantalizing Phantom Pita Chips. Inspired by the mysterious and adventurous spirit of the iconic show, these chips are a crunchy delight that will keep you munching through your own mysteries.

Serving: 4 servings

Preparation Time: 15 minutes
Ready Time: 25 minutes

Ingredients:
- 4 whole wheat pita bread rounds
- 2 tablespoons olive oil
- 1 teaspoon garlic powder
- 1 teaspoon onion powder
- 1 teaspoon smoked paprika
- 1/2 teaspoon cumin
- 1/2 teaspoon chili powder
- Salt and black pepper to taste

Instructions:
1. Preheat your oven to 375°F (190°C).
2. Cut each pita bread round into 8 wedges.
3. In a small bowl, mix together the olive oil, garlic powder, onion powder, smoked paprika, cumin, chili powder, salt, and black pepper.
4. Place the pita wedges on a baking sheet in a single layer.
5. Brush each wedge with the prepared spice-infused olive oil mixture, ensuring even coverage.
6. Bake in the preheated oven for 10-12 minutes or until the pita chips are golden brown and crispy.
7. Remove from the oven and let them cool for a few minutes.
8. Serve the Phantom Pita Chips with your favorite dip or enjoy them on their own as a spooky snack!

Nutrition Information:
- Serving Size: 1/4 of the recipe
- Calories: 120
- Total Fat: 6g
- Saturated Fat: 1g
- Trans Fat: 0g
- Cholesterol: 0mg
- Sodium: 220mg
- Total Carbohydrates: 15g
- Dietary Fiber: 2g
- Sugars: 1g
- Protein: 2g

Note: Nutritional values are approximate and may vary depending on specific ingredients and quantities used.

These Phantom Pita Chips are not only a delicious treat but also a perfect addition to any Scooby-Doo-inspired gathering. Enjoy the crunch and let the adventure begin!

43. Wicked Watermelon Slices

Step into the groovy world of Scooby-Doo with these Wicked Watermelon Slices! Inspired by the colorful and quirky adventures of Mystery Inc., these fruity delights are perfect for a refreshing snack or a groovy party treat. The vibrant colors and juicy flavors will have you saying, "Zoinks, these are delicious!"

Serving: Makes 8 servings.
Preparation Time: 15 minutes.
Ready Time: 2 hours (including chilling time).

Ingredients:
- 1 medium-sized watermelon
- 1 cup blueberries
- 1 cup strawberries, sliced
- 1 cup kiwi, peeled and sliced
- 1/4 cup fresh mint leaves, chopped
- 2 tablespoons honey

Instructions:
1. Prepare the Watermelon:
- Cut the watermelon into 1-inch thick slices.
- Use a Scooby-Doo-shaped cookie cutter to cut out watermelon shapes. Alternatively, you can cut the watermelon into triangles.
2. Arrange the Fruits:
- Place the watermelon slices on a serving platter.
- Decorate each watermelon slice with blueberries, sliced strawberries, and kiwi.
3. Drizzle with Honey:
- In a small bowl, mix the chopped mint leaves with honey.
- Drizzle the honey and mint mixture over the watermelon slices.

4. Chill:
- Place the watermelon slices in the refrigerator for at least 2 hours to allow the flavors to meld and the fruit to chill.

5. Serve:
- Remove the watermelon slices from the refrigerator just before serving.
- Enjoy these wicked watermelon slices with your favorite Scooby-Doo episode or as a fruity snack for your next gathering.

Nutrition Information:
(Per Serving)
- Calories: 120
- Total Fat: 0.5g
- Cholesterol: 0mg
- Sodium: 2mg
- Total Carbohydrates: 31g
- Dietary Fiber: 3g
- Sugars: 24g
- Protein: 2g

These Wicked Watermelon Slices are not only a treat for your taste buds but also a nod to the whimsical world of Scooby-Doo. Share them with your friends and family, and let the good times roll!

44. Shaggy's Scooby-Doo Stew

Step into the world of mystery-solving with Shaggy's Scooby-Doo Stew, a hearty and flavorful dish inspired by the iconic Scooby-Doo and his love for snacks. This stew captures the essence of the beloved cartoon with a medley of ingredients that would make even the hungriest detective and his Great Dane partner drool. Let the aroma of this simmering pot transport you to the spooky yet delicious adventures of the Mystery Inc. gang!

Serving: 4-6 servings
Preparation Time: 15 minutes
Ready Time: 1 hour

Ingredients:
- 1 lb boneless, skinless chicken thighs, diced

- 1 cup carrots, peeled and chopped
- 1 cup potatoes, diced
- 1 cup celery, chopped
- 1 onion, finely chopped
- 3 cloves garlic, minced
- 1 can (15 oz) diced tomatoes
- 4 cups chicken broth
- 1 cup frozen peas
- 1 cup corn kernels (fresh or frozen)
- 1 teaspoon dried thyme
- 1 teaspoon dried rosemary
- 1 bay leaf
- Salt and pepper to taste
- 2 tablespoons olive oil

Instructions:
1. In a large pot or Dutch oven, heat olive oil over medium heat. Add diced chicken thighs and cook until browned on all sides. Remove the chicken and set it aside.
2. In the same pot, add chopped onions and minced garlic. Sauté until the onions are translucent.
3. Add carrots, potatoes, and celery to the pot. Cook for 5 minutes, stirring occasionally.
4. Return the browned chicken to the pot and pour in the diced tomatoes with their juice. Stir to combine.
5. Pour in the chicken broth and add dried thyme, rosemary, bay leaf, salt, and pepper. Bring the stew to a simmer, then reduce the heat to low, cover, and let it cook for 30 minutes.
6. Add frozen peas and corn to the pot. Continue to simmer for an additional 15-20 minutes, or until the vegetables are tender.
7. Taste and adjust seasoning if necessary. Remove the bay leaf before serving.

Nutrition Information (per serving):
(Note: Nutritional values are approximate and may vary based on specific ingredients used.)
- Calories: 300
- Total Fat: 10g
- Saturated Fat: 2g
- Cholesterol: 80mg

- Sodium: 800mg
- Total Carbohydrates: 30g
- Dietary Fiber: 5g
- Sugars: 7g
- Protein: 25g

Warm your taste buds with Shaggy's Scooby-Doo Stew and embark on a culinary adventure that's as comforting as it is mysterious!

45. Velma's Veggie Wraps

Velma's Veggie Wraps are a nutritious and delicious homage to the brains behind Mystery Inc., Velma Dinkley. Packed with a medley of vibrant vegetables, these wraps are perfect for those who love a wholesome and satisfying meal. Just like Velma, these wraps are cleverly crafted, offering a mix of flavors and textures that will leave you feeling satisfied and ready for the next mystery-solving adventure.

Serving: Makes 4 wraps
Preparation Time: 15 minutes
Ready Time: 20 minutes

Ingredients:
- 4 large whole-grain or spinach tortillas
- 1 cup hummus
- 1 cucumber, thinly sliced
- 1 bell pepper (any color), thinly sliced
- 1 medium carrot, julienned
- 1 cup cherry tomatoes, halved
- 1 cup baby spinach leaves
- 1/2 red onion, thinly sliced
- 1 avocado, sliced
- 1/4 cup feta cheese, crumbled (optional)
- Fresh cilantro or parsley for garnish
- Salt and pepper to taste

Instructions:
1. Lay out the tortillas on a clean surface or plate.

2. Spread an even layer of hummus over each tortilla, leaving about a half-inch border around the edges.
3. In the center of each tortilla, layer the cucumber, bell pepper, carrot, cherry tomatoes, spinach, red onion, and avocado.
4. Optional: Sprinkle crumbled feta cheese over the veggies for an extra burst of flavor.
5. Season with salt and pepper to taste.
6. Carefully fold in the sides of the tortilla and then roll it up tightly from the bottom to form a wrap.
7. Repeat the process for the remaining tortillas.
8. Slice each wrap in half diagonally for a visually appealing presentation.
9. Garnish with fresh cilantro or parsley.
10. Serve immediately and enjoy the crunchy, fresh goodness of Velma's Veggie Wraps!

Nutrition Information:
(Per serving)
- Calories: 320
- Total Fat: 14g
- Saturated Fat: 2g
- Cholesterol: 0mg
- Sodium: 580mg
- Total Carbohydrates: 42g
- Dietary Fiber: 10g
- Sugars: 6g
- Protein: 10g

Note: Nutrition information is approximate and may vary based on specific ingredients used.

46. Daphne's Delicate Dessert Crepes

Indulge your taste buds in the whimsical world of Scooby-Doo with Daphne's Delicate Dessert Crepes. These delectable crepes are inspired by the elegance and sophistication of Daphne Blake, one of Mystery Inc.'s beloved members. Delight in every bite of these light, thin pancakes filled with a delightful array of sweet fillings. Perfect for breakfast, brunch, or a sweet treat any time of the day, these crepes are sure to transport you to the heart of mystery and adventure.

Serving: Makes 8 crepes
Preparation Time: 15 minutes
Ready Time: 30 minutes

Ingredients:
- 1 cup all-purpose flour
- 2 tablespoons sugar
- 1/4 teaspoon salt
- 1 1/2 cups milk
- 2 large eggs
- 2 tablespoons unsalted butter, melted
- 1 teaspoon vanilla extract

For the Filling:
- 1 cup fresh berries (strawberries, blueberries, raspberries)
- 1/2 cup whipped cream
- 2 tablespoons chocolate sauce
- Powdered sugar for dusting

Instructions:
1. In a blender, combine the flour, sugar, salt, milk, eggs, melted butter, and vanilla extract. Blend until the batter is smooth and well combined. Allow the batter to rest for at least 10 minutes.
2. Heat a non-stick skillet or crepe pan over medium heat. Lightly grease with butter or cooking spray.
3. Pour 1/4 cup of batter into the center of the skillet, swirling it to spread evenly and create a thin crepe. Cook for 1-2 minutes or until the edges begin to lightly brown.
4. Carefully flip the crepe using a spatula and cook the other side for an additional 1-2 minutes. Repeat until all the batter is used, stacking the crepes on a plate.
5. For the filling, spread a thin layer of whipped cream over each crepe. Add a handful of fresh berries and drizzle with chocolate sauce.
6. Fold the crepes into quarters or roll them, creating a beautiful presentation.
7. Dust the crepes with powdered sugar just before serving.

Nutrition Information:
Per Serving (1 crepe):
- Calories: 150

- Total Fat: 7g
- Saturated Fat: 4g
- Cholesterol: 65mg
- Sodium: 100mg
- Total Carbohydrates: 18g
- Dietary Fiber: 1g
- Sugars: 7g
- Protein: 4g

Delight in the mystery-solving spirit of Scooby-Doo with these elegant and delicious dessert crepes inspired by Daphne herself. Enjoy the sweetness and excitement of these delicate treats that are sure to satisfy your taste buds and transport you to the world of mystery and fun!

47. Fred's Fruit Salsa

Step into the world of mystery and intrigue with Fred's Fruit Salsa, a delightful concoction inspired by Scooby-Doo's adventures. This vibrant salsa is a perfect blend of fresh fruits and zesty flavors, adding a touch of excitement to your culinary escapades. Whether you're hosting a Scooby-Doo marathon or just craving a healthy and delicious snack, Fred's Fruit Salsa is sure to tantalize your taste buds with every bite.

Serving: 4 servings
Preparation Time: 15 minutes
Ready Time: 15 minutes

Ingredients:
- 1 cup diced fresh pineapple
- 1 cup diced mango
- 1 cup diced strawberries
- 1/2 cup diced red onion
- 1/4 cup finely chopped fresh cilantro
- 1 jalapeño, seeds removed and finely chopped
- Juice of 2 limes
- 1 tablespoon honey
- Salt to taste
- 1 bag of your favorite tortilla chips for serving

Instructions:
1. In a large bowl, combine the diced pineapple, mango, strawberries, red onion, cilantro, and jalapeño.
2. In a small bowl, whisk together the lime juice, honey, and a pinch of salt.
3. Pour the lime-honey mixture over the fruit mixture and gently toss until well combined. Adjust salt to taste.
4. Allow the salsa to marinate for at least 10 minutes to let the flavors meld together.
5. Serve Fred's Fruit Salsa with your favorite tortilla chips and enjoy the vibrant burst of flavors.

Nutrition Information:
Note: Nutrition information is approximate and may vary based on specific ingredients used.
- Serving Size: 1/4 of the recipe
- Calories: 120
- Total Fat: 0.5g
- Saturated Fat: 0g
- Cholesterol: 0mg
- Sodium: 50mg
- Total Carbohydrates: 30g
- Dietary Fiber: 3g
- Sugars: 20g
- Protein: 1g

Embrace the spirit of Scooby-Doo's adventures with Fred's Fruit Salsa—a refreshing and healthy treat that's perfect for any occasion.

48. Haunted Hamburger Sliders

Step into the spooky world of Scooby-Doo with these "Haunted Hamburger Sliders," a ghoulishly delightful twist on the classic slider. Inspired by the mysterious and fun-filled adventures of Scooby and the gang, these sliders are perfect for a Scooby-Doo-themed gathering or a haunted movie night. Get ready to sink your teeth into a deliciously eerie experience that even Shaggy and Scooby would approve of!

Serving: Makes approximately 12 haunted hamburger sliders.

Preparation Time: 15 minutes
Ready Time: 30 minutes

Ingredients:
- 1 pound ground beef
- 1/2 cup breadcrumbs
- 1/4 cup finely chopped onion
- 1/4 cup ketchup
- 1 tablespoon Worcestershire sauce
- 1 teaspoon garlic powder
- Salt and pepper to taste
- 12 small slider buns
- 1 cup shredded cheddar cheese
- 24 edible googly eyes
- Ketchup and mustard for garnish (optional)

Instructions:
1. Preheat your grill or stovetop pan over medium-high heat.
2. In a large bowl, combine ground beef, breadcrumbs, chopped onion, ketchup, Worcestershire sauce, garlic powder, salt, and pepper. Mix well until all ingredients are evenly incorporated.
3. Divide the mixture into 12 portions and shape them into small burger patties.
4. Grill the patties for 3-4 minutes per side or until they reach your desired level of doneness.
5. In the last minute of cooking, sprinkle shredded cheddar cheese on each patty and close the grill lid to melt the cheese.
6. Place the cheesy patties on the slider buns.
7. Create a spooky face on each slider using edible googly eyes. You can use ketchup and mustard to add extra details if desired.
8. Serve your Haunted Hamburger Sliders on a platter and watch them disappear as mysteriously as a ghost in the night!

Nutrition Information:
Note: Nutrition information is per slider.
- Calories: 180
- Total Fat: 9g
- Saturated Fat: 4g
- Cholesterol: 30mg
- Sodium: 200mg

- Total Carbohydrates: 13g
- Dietary Fiber: 1g
- Sugars: 2g
- Protein: 11g

These Haunted Hamburger Sliders are sure to add a spooky touch to your Scooby-Doo-inspired feast. Enjoy the combination of flavors and the playful appearance that pays homage to the beloved animated series!

49. Creepy Crawly Rice Krispies Treats

Step into the spooky and kooky world of Scooby-Doo with our "Creepy Crawly Rice Krispies Treats"! Inspired by the mysterious and thrilling adventures of Scooby and the gang, these treats are perfect for a Halloween party or any Scooby-Doo-themed gathering. The classic Rice Krispies Treats get a whimsical twist with creepy-crawly decorations that will have everyone exclaiming, "Zoinks!"

Serving: Makes 12 spooky treats
Preparation Time: 15 minutes
Ready Time: 1 hour (including chilling time)

Ingredients:
- 3 tablespoons unsalted butter
- 1 package (10 ounces) marshmallows
- 6 cups Rice Krispies cereal
- 1 cup chocolate chips
- 1 cup pretzel sticks
- 1/2 cup gummy worms
- 1/4 cup candy eyes

Instructions:
1. In a large saucepan, melt the butter over low heat. Add the marshmallows and stir until completely melted and well combined.
2. Remove the saucepan from the heat and add the Rice Krispies cereal. Stir until the cereal is evenly coated with the marshmallow mixture.
3. Press the mixture into a greased 9x13-inch baking dish using a greased spatula or your hands. Allow it to cool slightly.

4. In a microwave-safe bowl, melt the chocolate chips in 30-second intervals, stirring between each interval until smooth.
5. Drizzle the melted chocolate over the Rice Krispies treats to create a spooky web-like pattern.
6. Break the pretzel sticks in half and insert them into the treats to resemble legs. Place gummy worms strategically on the treats and add candy eyes for an extra creepy effect.
7. Allow the treats to cool completely and the chocolate to set, approximately 1 hour.
8. Once set, cut the treats into squares or rectangles and serve them up to your guests with a side of mystery and excitement!

Nutrition Information:
(Per serving - 1 treat)
- Calories: 220
- Total Fat: 7g
- Saturated Fat: 4g
- Cholesterol: 10mg
- Sodium: 120mg
- Total Carbohydrates: 38g
- Dietary Fiber: 1g
- Sugars: 20g
- Protein: 2g

Unmask the fun with these Creepy Crawly Rice Krispies Treats inspired by Scooby-Doo, and watch as they vanish from the snack table in no time!

50. Ghostly Gingerbread Cookies

Nothing says mystery-solving fun like a batch of Ghostly Gingerbread Cookies inspired by Scooby-Doo! These spooky yet delicious treats are perfect for any Scooby-Doo-themed party or a spooky movie night. Get ready to bake up some ghostly delights that even the bravest of detectives won't be able to resist.

Serving: Makes about 24 cookies
Preparation Time: 30 minutes
Ready Time: 2 hours (includes chilling time)

Ingredients:
- 3 cups all-purpose flour
- 1 teaspoon baking powder
- 1/2 teaspoon baking soda
- 1/4 teaspoon salt
- 1 tablespoon ground ginger
- 2 teaspoons ground cinnamon
- 1/2 teaspoon ground cloves
- 1/2 teaspoon ground nutmeg
- 3/4 cup unsalted butter, softened
- 1/2 cup packed brown sugar
- 1 large egg
- 1/2 cup molasses
- 1 teaspoon vanilla extract
- Ghost-shaped cookie cutter
- White icing or frosting (for decorating)

Instructions:
1. In a bowl, whisk together the flour, baking powder, baking soda, salt, ginger, cinnamon, cloves, and nutmeg. Set aside.
2. In a separate large mixing bowl, cream the softened butter and brown sugar until light and fluffy. Add the egg, molasses, and vanilla extract, mixing until well combined.
3. Gradually add the dry ingredients to the wet ingredients, mixing until a dough forms. Divide the dough in half, shape each half into a disk, wrap them in plastic wrap, and refrigerate for at least 1 hour or until firm.
4. Preheat your oven to 350°F (175°C). Line baking sheets with parchment paper.
5. Roll out one disk of dough on a lightly floured surface to about 1/4-inch thickness. Use the ghost-shaped cookie cutter to cut out cookies and carefully transfer them to the prepared baking sheets, leaving space between each cookie.
6. Bake the cookies for 8-10 minutes or until the edges are firm. Allow the cookies to cool on the baking sheets for a few minutes before transferring them to a wire rack to cool completely.
7. Once the cookies are completely cooled, decorate them using white icing or frosting to create ghostly faces or designs. Let the icing set before serving.

Nutrition Information (per serving, based on 1 cookie):
- Calories: 120
- Total Fat: 5g
- Saturated Fat: 3g
- Cholesterol: 18mg
- Sodium: 70mg
- Total Carbohydrate: 18g
- Dietary Fiber: 0.5g
- Sugars: 8g
- Protein: 1.5g

Enjoy these Ghostly Gingerbread Cookies while you unmask mysteries or share them with friends during your next Scooby-Doo adventure!

51. Werewolf Walnut Brownies

Sink your teeth into these delectable Werewolf Walnut Brownies inspired by Scooby-Doo! With a howlingly good combination of rich chocolate, crunchy walnuts, and a mysterious swirl, these brownies will have you feeling like you're solving a mystery with the gang.

Serving: Makes 12-16 brownies
Preparation Time: 15 minutes
Ready Time: 40 minutes

Ingredients:
- 1 cup unsalted butter
- 1 cup granulated sugar
- 1 cup brown sugar
- 4 large eggs
- 1 tablespoon vanilla extract
- 1 cup all-purpose flour
- 1 cup cocoa powder
- 1 teaspoon baking powder
- 1/2 teaspoon salt
- 1 cup chopped walnuts
- 1/2 cup chocolate chips
- Red food coloring

Instructions:
1. Preheat your oven to 350°F (175°C) and line a 9x13-inch baking pan with parchment paper.
2. In a microwave-safe bowl, melt the butter in 30-second intervals until fully melted. Allow it to cool slightly.
3. In a separate bowl, whisk together the granulated sugar, brown sugar, eggs, and vanilla extract until well combined.
4. Slowly pour the melted butter into the egg mixture while whisking continuously.
5. In another bowl, sift together the flour, cocoa powder, baking powder, and salt. Gradually add this dry mixture to the wet ingredients, stirring until just combined.
6. Fold in the chopped walnuts and chocolate chips.
7. Pour the brownie batter into the prepared baking pan, spreading it evenly.
8. Now for the werewolf swirl: mix a few drops of red food coloring into a small amount of batter in a separate bowl until you achieve a deep red color. Use a spoon to drizzle the red batter over the brownie batter in the pan.
9. Use a toothpick or knife to gently swirl the red batter into the brownie batter, creating a marbled effect resembling a werewolf's howl.
10. Bake in the preheated oven for 25-30 minutes or until a toothpick inserted in the center comes out with a few moist crumbs.
11. Once baked, allow the brownies to cool completely in the pan before slicing into squares.

Nutrition Information (per serving, assuming 12 servings):
- Calories: 420
- Total Fat: 24g
- Saturated Fat: 12g
- Cholesterol: 105mg
- Sodium: 210mg
- Total Carbohydrate: 50g
- Dietary Fiber: 3g
- Sugars: 37g
- Protein: 6g

These Werewolf Walnut Brownies are best enjoyed with friends or as a snack while unraveling mysterious adventures, just like Scooby-Doo and the gang!

52. Mummy Meatball Subs

'Solving mysteries with Scooby-Doo and the gang can really work up an appetite, and there's no better way to satisfy it than with these 'Mummy Meatball Subs'. Inspired by the adventures of unearthing hidden treasures and solving puzzling mysteries, these flavorful subs will transport you to the heart of the mystery-solving action. Delicious, hearty, and easy to make, they're a perfect addition to any Scooby-Doo-themed feast!"

Serving: Makes 4 servings.
Preparation Time: 20 minutes.
Ready Time: 40 minutes.

Ingredients:
- 1 pound ground beef
- 1/2 cup bread crumbs
- 1/4 cup grated Parmesan cheese
- 1 egg
- 1 teaspoon dried oregano
- 1 teaspoon dried basil
- 1/2 teaspoon garlic powder
- Salt and pepper to taste
- 1 tablespoon olive oil
- 1 jar (24 ounces) marinara sauce
- 4 hoagie/sub rolls
- 8 slices mozzarella cheese
- Sliced black olives for garnish (optional)

Instructions:
1. Preheat your oven to 375°F (190°C).
2. In a mixing bowl, combine the ground beef, bread crumbs, Parmesan cheese, egg, oregano, basil, garlic powder, salt, and pepper. Mix until well combined.
3. Form the mixture into meatballs, about 1 inch in diameter.
4. Heat olive oil in a skillet over medium heat. Brown the meatballs on all sides, about 5 minutes.

5. Pour the marinara sauce into the skillet with the meatballs. Simmer for 10-15 minutes until the meatballs are cooked through and the sauce thickens slightly.
6. Slice the hoagie rolls in half lengthwise and place them on a baking sheet.
7. Place two slices of mozzarella cheese on each roll.
8. Using a slotted spoon, place the meatballs onto the rolls, dividing them evenly among the subs.
9. Spoon some marinara sauce over the meatballs on each roll.
10. Top with additional mozzarella cheese if desired and sliced black olives for a 'mummy' effect.
11. Bake in the preheated oven for about 10 minutes or until the cheese is melted and bubbly.
12. Remove from the oven and serve hot, enjoying these mummy-inspired meatball subs!

Nutrition Information:
Note: Nutritional values are approximate and may vary based on specific ingredients used.
- Calories per serving: Approximately 560 calories
- Total Fat: 28g
- Saturated Fat: 12g
- Cholesterol: 130mg
- Sodium: 1180mg
- Total Carbohydrates: 38g
- Dietary Fiber: 3g
- Sugars: 7g
- Protein: 36g

These 'Mummy Meatball Subs' are a scrumptious homage to Scooby-Doo's adventures, and they're sure to please fans of all ages!

53. Frankenfruit Salad

Step into the world of mystery and nostalgia with the "Frankenfruit Salad," a delightful concoction inspired by the iconic Scooby-Doo and his gang of mystery-solving friends. This salad is a medley of vibrant and fresh fruits, bringing a playful twist to your table that even Scooby and

Shaggy would find irresistible. Packed with flavor and goodness, it's a healthy treat that's perfect for any occasion!

Serving: 4 servings
Preparation Time: 15 minutes
Ready Time: 15 minutes

Ingredients:
- 2 cups strawberries, hulled and halved
- 1 cup blueberries
- 1 cup green grapes, halved
- 1 cup pineapple chunks
- 1 cup kiwi, peeled and sliced
- 1 cup orange segments
- 1/2 cup honey, for the dressing
- 1 tablespoon lime juice
- 1 teaspoon poppy seeds
- 1/4 cup chopped mint leaves, for garnish

Instructions:
1. In a large mixing bowl, combine the strawberries, blueberries, green grapes, pineapple chunks, kiwi slices, and orange segments. Gently toss to mix the fruits evenly.
2. In a small bowl, whisk together the honey, lime juice, and poppy seeds to create the dressing.
3. Pour the dressing over the mixed fruits and toss until the fruits are evenly coated.
4. Allow the salad to chill in the refrigerator for at least 10 minutes to enhance the flavors.
5. Just before serving, garnish the Frankenfruit Salad with chopped mint leaves for a refreshing finish.

Nutrition Information:
Note: Nutrition information is approximate and may vary based on specific ingredients used.
- Calories: 120 per serving
- Total Fat: 1g
- Cholesterol: 0mg
- Sodium: 5mg
- Total Carbohydrates: 30g

- Dietary Fiber: 5g
- Sugars: 20g
- Protein: 2g

Unveil the mystery behind this Frankenfruit Salad, a tribute to the classic Scooby-Doo adventures that will leave your taste buds craving more. It's a healthy and delicious way to enjoy the magic of Scooby and the gang at your dining table!

54. Zombie Zucchini Muffins

Get ready to embark on a culinary adventure with the Mystery Inc. gang! Inspired by the spooky and kooky world of Scooby-Doo, these Zombie Zucchini Muffins are a ghoulishly delightful treat that will have you saying, "Zoinks!" Packed with the goodness of zucchini and a hint of mystery, these muffins are perfect for breakfast, snacks, or even a midnight snack during your next mystery-solving escapade.

Serving: Makes 12 muffins
Preparation Time: 15 minutes
Ready Time: 35 minutes

Ingredients:
- 2 cups grated zucchini
- 1 1/2 cups all-purpose flour
- 1/2 cup whole wheat flour
- 1 teaspoon baking powder
- 1/2 teaspoon baking soda
- 1/2 teaspoon salt
- 1 teaspoon ground cinnamon
- 1/2 teaspoon ground nutmeg
- 1/4 teaspoon ground cloves
- 1/2 cup unsalted butter, melted
- 1/2 cup brown sugar, packed
- 1/4 cup granulated sugar
- 2 large eggs
- 1 teaspoon vanilla extract
- 1/2 cup chopped walnuts (optional)
- 1/2 cup raisins (optional)

Instructions:
1. Preheat your oven to 350°F (175°C). Grease a muffin tin or line it with paper liners.
2. In a large bowl, combine the grated zucchini, melted butter, brown sugar, granulated sugar, eggs, and vanilla extract. Mix well until the ingredients are thoroughly combined.
3. In a separate bowl, whisk together the all-purpose flour, whole wheat flour, baking powder, baking soda, salt, cinnamon, nutmeg, and cloves.
4. Gradually add the dry ingredients to the zucchini mixture, stirring until just combined. If desired, fold in the chopped walnuts and raisins.
5. Spoon the batter into the prepared muffin tin, filling each cup about two-thirds full.
6. Bake in the preheated oven for 20-25 minutes or until a toothpick inserted into the center of a muffin comes out clean.
7. Allow the muffins to cool in the tin for 5 minutes, then transfer them to a wire rack to cool completely.

Nutrition Information:
(Per serving - 1 muffin)
- Calories: 200
- Total Fat: 9g
- Saturated Fat: 5g
- Cholesterol: 45mg
- Sodium: 180mg
- Total Carbohydrates: 27g
- Dietary Fiber: 2g
- Sugars: 12g
- Protein: 4g

Unmask the deliciousness of these Zombie Zucchini Muffins and enjoy a spooktacular treat that even Scooby and Shaggy would approve of!

55. Vampire Vanilla Cupcakes

Indulge your sweet tooth with a bewitching treat inspired by the mysterious and mischievous adventures of Scooby-Doo! These Vampire Vanilla Cupcakes are sure to cast a spell on your taste buds with their decadent vanilla flavor and hauntingly delicious frosting. Whether you're solving mysteries with the Mystery Inc. gang or simply satisfying your dessert cravings, these cupcakes are a fang-tastic choice!

Serving: Makes 12 cupcakes
Preparation Time: 15 minutes
Ready Time: 35 minutes

Ingredients:
- 1 1/2 cups all-purpose flour
- 1 1/2 teaspoons baking powder
- 1/2 teaspoon baking soda
- 1/4 teaspoon salt
- 1/2 cup unsalted butter, softened
- 1 cup granulated sugar
- 2 large eggs
- 1 teaspoon vanilla extract
- 1 cup buttermilk

For the Vampire Vanilla Frosting:
- 1 cup unsalted butter, softened
- 4 cups powdered sugar
- 1/4 cup whole milk
- 2 teaspoons vanilla extract
- Red food coloring (to achieve the vampire blood color)

Instructions:
1. Preheat the oven:
Preheat your oven to 350°F (175°C). Line a cupcake tin with paper liners.
2. Prepare the dry ingredients:
In a medium bowl, whisk together the flour, baking powder, baking soda, and salt. Set aside.
3. Cream the butter and sugar:
In a large mixing bowl, cream together the softened butter and granulated sugar until light and fluffy.
4. Add eggs and vanilla:
Beat in the eggs one at a time, ensuring each is fully incorporated. Add the vanilla extract and mix well.
5. Alternate dry ingredients and buttermilk:

Gradually add the dry ingredients to the wet ingredients, alternating with buttermilk. Begin and end with the dry ingredients, mixing until just combined.

6. Fill cupcake liners:

Divide the batter evenly among the cupcake liners, filling each about two-thirds full.

7. Bake:

Bake in the preheated oven for 18-20 minutes or until a toothpick inserted into the center comes out clean. Allow the cupcakes to cool completely on a wire rack.

8. Prepare the Vampire Vanilla Frosting:

In a large bowl, beat together the softened butter, powdered sugar, milk, and vanilla extract until smooth and creamy. Add red food coloring until you achieve the desired vampire blood color.

9. Frost the cupcakes:

Once the cupcakes are completely cooled, frost them with the Vampire Vanilla Frosting using a piping bag or a spatula.

10. Serve and enjoy:

Sink your teeth into these delightful Vampire Vanilla Cupcakes and savor the enchanting flavor inspired by Scooby-Doo's supernatural escapades!

Nutrition Information:
(Per Cupcake)
- Calories: 320
- Total Fat: 16g
- Saturated Fat: 10g
- Cholesterol: 65mg
- Sodium: 180mg
- Total Carbohydrates: 42g
- Sugars: 30g
- Protein: 2g

Note: Nutrition information is approximate and may vary based on specific ingredients and quantities used.

56. Goblin Gazpacho

Get ready to embark on a culinary adventure inspired by the mysterious world of Scooby-Doo! Our "Goblin Gazpacho" is a spooky twist on the classic Spanish soup, perfect for those ghost-chasing moments when you need a refreshing and flavorful dish. Packed with vibrant vegetables and a hint of mystery, this gazpacho is sure to satisfy both your hunger and your curiosity.

Serving: 4 servings
Preparation Time: 15 minutes
Ready Time: 2 hours (including chilling time)

Ingredients:
- 6 ripe tomatoes, chopped
- 1 cucumber, peeled and diced
- 1 red bell pepper, diced
- 1 green bell pepper, diced
- 1 small red onion, finely chopped
- 3 cloves garlic, minced
- 4 cups tomato juice
- 1/4 cup red wine vinegar
- 1/4 cup olive oil
- 1 teaspoon salt
- 1/2 teaspoon black pepper
- 1 teaspoon sugar
- 1 teaspoon hot sauce (adjust to taste)
- 1/2 teaspoon ground cumin
- 1/2 teaspoon paprika
- Fresh basil leaves for garnish

Instructions:
1. In a blender or food processor, combine the chopped tomatoes, cucumber, red bell pepper, green bell pepper, red onion, and garlic. Pulse until the vegetables are finely chopped but not pureed.
2. Transfer the vegetable mixture to a large bowl and add the tomato juice, red wine vinegar, olive oil, salt, black pepper, sugar, hot sauce, cumin, and paprika. Mix well to combine.
3. Cover the bowl and refrigerate the gazpacho for at least 2 hours to allow the flavors to meld and the soup to chill.
4. Before serving, taste and adjust the seasoning if necessary. Add more salt, pepper, or hot sauce according to your preference.
5. Ladle the chilled Goblin Gazpacho into bowls and garnish with fresh basil leaves.

6. Serve alongside crusty bread or your favorite Scooby snacks for a complete and satisfying meal.

Nutrition Information:
(Per Serving)
- Calories: 180
- Total Fat: 11g
- Saturated Fat: 1.5g
- Cholesterol: 0mg
- Sodium: 700mg
- Total Carbohydrates: 20g
- Dietary Fiber: 4g
- Sugars: 12g
- Protein: 3g

Unmask the deliciousness of our Goblin Gazpacho as you enjoy this flavorful and chilling soup inspired by the adventures of Scooby-Doo and the gang!

57. Ghoulish Greek Yogurt Parfait

Transport yourself to the spooky world of Scooby-Doo with this delightfully haunting treat—Ghoulish Greek Yogurt Parfait. A concoction inspired by the mystery-solving adventures of the Scooby-Doo gang, this parfait combines the goodness of Greek yogurt with a medley of eerie toppings. Perfect for a Scooby-Doo marathon or a Halloween-themed gathering, this chillingly delicious parfait is sure to please your taste buds while keeping you on the edge of your seat.

Serving: Serves 4
Preparation Time: 15 minutes
Ready Time: 15 minutes

Ingredients:
- 2 cups Greek yogurt
- 1/4 cup honey
- 1 teaspoon vanilla extract
- 1 cup granola
- 1 cup mixed berries (strawberries, blueberries, raspberries)

- 1/2 cup dark chocolate chips
- 1/4 cup shredded coconut
- 1/4 cup sliced almonds
- Gummy worms (for a spooky touch)
- Fresh mint leaves (for garnish)

Instructions:
1. In a mixing bowl, combine Greek yogurt, honey, and vanilla extract. Mix well until smooth and creamy.
2. In serving glasses or bowls, start by layering a spoonful of the Greek yogurt mixture at the bottom.
3. Add a layer of granola, followed by a layer of mixed berries.
4. Sprinkle dark chocolate chips, shredded coconut, and sliced almonds over the berries.
5. Repeat the layers until the glass or bowl is filled, finishing with a dollop of the Greek yogurt mixture on top.
6. Garnish with gummy worms for a spooky twist and fresh mint leaves for a burst of color.
7. Serve immediately and enjoy the chillingly delightful Ghoulish Greek Yogurt Parfait!

Nutrition Information (per serving):
- Calories: 320
- Protein: 15g
- Fat: 15g
- Carbohydrates: 35g
- Fiber: 5g
- Sugar: 20g
- Calcium: 20% DV
- Iron: 10% DV

Note: Nutrition information is approximate and may vary based on specific ingredients used. Adjust quantities according to individual dietary preferences and restrictions.

58. Phantom Pumpkin Soup

Embark on a culinary adventure with our "Phantom Pumpkin Soup," inspired by the mysterious and thrilling world of Scooby-Doo. This velvety and flavorful soup captures the essence of the spooky and fun atmosphere that the gang encounters during their investigations. Unmask the secrets hidden within this hearty pumpkin concoction and treat your taste buds to a taste of mystery and nostalgia.

Serving: 4 servings
Preparation Time: 15 minutes
Ready Time: 45 minutes

Ingredients:
- 1 medium-sized pumpkin, peeled and diced
- 1 onion, finely chopped
- 2 cloves garlic, minced
- 2 carrots, peeled and chopped
- 2 tablespoons olive oil
- 4 cups vegetable broth
- 1 teaspoon ground cumin
- 1/2 teaspoon ground coriander
- 1/2 teaspoon smoked paprika
- Salt and pepper to taste
- 1 cup coconut milk
- Fresh parsley for garnish

Instructions:
1. Prepare the Pumpkin:
- Peel and dice the medium-sized pumpkin. Remove the seeds and set aside.
2. Sauté Aromatics:
- In a large pot, heat olive oil over medium heat. Add finely chopped onions and minced garlic. Sauté until the onions are translucent.
3. Add Vegetables:
- Add the diced pumpkin and chopped carrots to the pot. Sauté for 5-7 minutes until the vegetables begin to soften.
4. Season the Soup:
- Sprinkle ground cumin, ground coriander, smoked paprika, salt, and pepper over the vegetables. Stir to coat the vegetables in the spices.
5. Simmer:
- Pour in the vegetable broth and bring the mixture to a boil. Reduce the heat to low, cover the pot, and let it simmer for 25-30 minutes or until the pumpkin is tender.

6. Blend the Soup:
- Using an immersion blender, carefully blend the soup until smooth. Alternatively, transfer the soup to a blender in batches, blending until smooth.

7. Add Coconut Milk:
- Stir in the coconut milk, allowing the soup to simmer for an additional 5-10 minutes to combine the flavors.

8. Adjust Seasoning:
- Taste the soup and adjust the seasoning if necessary. Add more salt and pepper to suit your preferences.

9. Serve:
- Ladle the Phantom Pumpkin Soup into bowls. Garnish with fresh parsley for a burst of color and freshness.

Nutrition Information:
(Per Serving)
- Calories: 220
- Total Fat: 12g
- Saturated Fat: 6g
- Cholesterol: 0mg
- Sodium: 800mg
- Total Carbohydrates: 28g
- Dietary Fiber: 6g
- Sugars: 8g
- Protein: 4g

Uncover the mystery behind the delectable Phantom Pumpkin Soup and enjoy a warm and satisfying dish that pays homage to the timeless adventures of Scooby-Doo and the gang.

59. Swampy Spinach Artichoke Dip

Get ready to embark on a culinary adventure with Scooby-Doo and the gang! In this cookbook inspired by everyone's favorite mystery-solving crew, we bring you "Swampy Spinach Artichoke Dip." This ooey-gooey concoction is sure to delight your taste buds and transport you to the heart of a mysterious swamp. Scooby and Shaggy would undoubtedly approve of this cheesy, savory dip that's perfect for sharing during your next Scooby-Doo marathon.

Serving: Makes approximately 8 servings.
Preparation Time: 15 minutes
Ready Time: 30 minutes

Ingredients:
- 1 cup frozen chopped spinach, thawed and drained
- 1 cup canned artichoke hearts, drained and chopped
- 1 cup mayonnaise
- 1 cup sour cream
- 1 cup shredded mozzarella cheese
- 1 cup grated Parmesan cheese
- 1 teaspoon garlic powder
- 1 teaspoon onion powder
- 1/2 teaspoon salt
- 1/2 teaspoon black pepper
- 1/4 teaspoon cayenne pepper (optional, for a hint of heat)
- 1 tablespoon olive oil
- Tortilla chips or sliced baguette, for serving

Instructions:
1. Preheat your oven to 375°F (190°C).
2. In a medium-sized mixing bowl, combine the thawed and drained chopped spinach, chopped artichoke hearts, mayonnaise, sour cream, mozzarella cheese, Parmesan cheese, garlic powder, onion powder, salt, black pepper, and cayenne pepper (if using). Mix everything together until well combined.
3. Heat olive oil in a skillet over medium heat. Add the spinach and artichoke mixture to the skillet and cook for about 5 minutes, stirring occasionally, until the cheese is melted and the mixture is heated through.
4. Transfer the mixture to a baking dish and spread it evenly.
5. Bake in the preheated oven for approximately 20-25 minutes or until the top is golden brown and bubbly.
6. Remove from the oven and let it cool slightly before serving.
7. Serve the Swampy Spinach Artichoke Dip with tortilla chips or sliced baguette for dipping.

Nutrition Information:
(Per Serving)

- Calories: 320
- Total Fat: 28g
- Saturated Fat: 10g
- Trans Fat: 0g
- Cholesterol: 45mg
- Sodium: 600mg
- Total Carbohydrates: 7g
- Dietary Fiber: 2g
- Sugars: 2g
- Protein: 10g

Enjoy your Scooby-Doo-inspired culinary creation – a dip that's as mysterious and delicious as the adventures of Scooby and the gang!

60. Monster Mash Mashed Potatoes

Join Scooby-Doo and the gang on a spooktacular culinary adventure with our "Monster Mash Mashed Potatoes" recipe! Inspired by the mysterious and fun-filled world of Scooby-Doo, these mashed potatoes are a delightful twist on a classic comfort dish. Packed with flavor and a hint of mystery, this dish is sure to satisfy both your taste buds and your appetite for adventure.

Serving: 4 servings
Preparation Time: 15 minutes
Ready Time: 30 minutes

Ingredients:
- 4 large russet potatoes, peeled and cut into chunks
- 1/2 cup unsalted butter
- 1/2 cup milk
- 1 cup shredded cheddar cheese
- 1/4 cup sour cream
- 1 teaspoon garlic powder
- Salt and pepper to taste
- Chives or green onions, chopped (for garnish)

Instructions:

1. Boil the Potatoes: Place the peeled and chopped potatoes in a large pot of salted water. Bring to a boil and cook until the potatoes are fork-tender, about 15-20 minutes.
2. Mash the Potatoes: Drain the potatoes and return them to the pot. Add the butter, milk, shredded cheddar cheese, sour cream, garlic powder, salt, and pepper. Mash the potatoes until smooth and creamy.
3. Adjust Seasoning: Taste the mashed potatoes and adjust the seasoning, adding more salt and pepper if needed.
4. Serve with a Scooby-Doo Twist: Scoop the mashed potatoes onto plates, forming them into spooky shapes if desired. Top with extra shredded cheddar cheese and garnish with chopped chives or green onions for a pop of color.
5. Enjoy the Mystery Mash: Serve these Monster Mash Mashed Potatoes alongside your favorite Scooby-Doo episodes or movies for an extra-special dining experience.

Nutrition Information (per serving):
- Calories: 350
- Protein: 8g
- Fat: 20g
- Carbohydrates: 35g
- Fiber: 3g
- Sugar: 2g
- Sodium: 120mg

Unmask the deliciousness with this easy-to-make Monster Mash Mashed Potatoes recipe – a perfect addition to your Scooby-Doo-inspired cookbook!

61. Shiver-inducing Sherbet

Step into the world of mystery and laughter with our "Shiver-inducing Sherbet," a delightful treat inspired by the iconic adventures of Scooby-Doo and the gang. This chillingly delicious sherbet is sure to transport you back to those spine-tingling moments when the gang unmasked the villain. Get ready for a taste bud adventure that's as exciting as solving a mystery!

Serving: Makes 6 servings

Preparation Time: 15 minutes
Ready Time: 4 hours (including freezing time)

Ingredients:
- 2 cups frozen mixed berries (strawberries, blueberries, raspberries)
- 1 cup orange juice
- 1/2 cup sugar
- 1 tablespoon lemon juice
- 1 teaspoon orange zest
- 2 cups plain yogurt
- 1 teaspoon vanilla extract
- 1/2 cup whipped cream (for garnish)
- Fresh berries and mint leaves (for garnish)

Instructions:
1. Prepare the Berry Mixture:
- In a blender, combine the frozen mixed berries, orange juice, sugar, lemon juice, and orange zest. Blend until smooth.
2. Strain the Mixture:
- Strain the berry mixture through a fine mesh sieve into a bowl to remove any seeds or pulp. This will give your sherbet a smooth and creamy texture.
3. Mix in Yogurt and Vanilla:
- In the same bowl, add the plain yogurt and vanilla extract to the strained berry mixture. Mix until well combined.
4. Chill the Mixture:
- Place the mixture in the refrigerator for about 1 hour to chill.
5. Freeze the Sherbet:
- Transfer the chilled mixture into an ice cream maker and churn according to the manufacturer's instructions. If you don't have an ice cream maker, you can pour the mixture into a shallow dish and freeze, stirring every 30 minutes until set.
6. Serve and Garnish:
- Once the sherbet is frozen, scoop it into bowls or cones. Top with a dollop of whipped cream and garnish with fresh berries and mint leaves.
7. Enjoy the Shiver-inducing Sherbet:
- Dive into the world of Scooby-Doo as you savor each spoonful of this chilling sherbet. Don't forget to share with friends, just like Scooby and the gang would!

Nutrition Information:
Note: Nutrition information is approximate and may vary based on specific ingredients used.
- Calories per serving: 180
- Total Fat: 5g
- Cholesterol: 15mg
- Sodium: 45mg
- Total Carbohydrates: 30g
- Dietary Fiber: 3g
- Sugars: 25g
- Protein: 6g

Embark on a flavor-filled adventure with our Shiver-inducing Sherbet, a perfect addition to your Scooby-Doo-inspired culinary journey!

62. Witches' Whirlwind Wraps

Embark on a culinary adventure inspired by the whimsical world of Scooby-Doo with our enchanting recipe for Witches' Whirlwind Wraps! These tantalizing wraps are as mysterious and delightful as the spooky capers our favorite gang encounters. Packed with flavorful ingredients and a touch of magic, these wraps are sure to cast a spell on your taste buds.

Serving: 4 wraps
Preparation Time: 15 minutes
Ready Time: 30 minutes

Ingredients:
- 4 large flour tortillas
- 1 pound boneless, skinless chicken breasts, cooked and shredded
- 1 cup black beans, drained and rinsed
- 1 cup corn kernels (fresh or frozen)
- 1 cup shredded cheddar cheese
- 1/2 cup diced tomatoes
- 1/4 cup diced red onion
- 1/4 cup chopped fresh cilantro
- 1/4 cup sliced black olives
- 1/4 cup sour cream

- 1/4 cup salsa
- 1 teaspoon ground cumin
- 1 teaspoon chili powder
- Salt and pepper to taste

Instructions:
1. In a large mixing bowl, combine the shredded chicken, black beans, corn, cumin, chili powder, salt, and pepper. Toss the mixture until well combined and set aside.
2. Heat the flour tortillas in a dry skillet or microwave until warm and pliable.
3. Lay out each tortilla and evenly distribute the chicken mixture in the center of each.
4. Sprinkle shredded cheddar cheese over the chicken mixture on each tortilla.
5. Add diced tomatoes, red onion, cilantro, and black olives on top of the cheese.
6. Drizzle a dollop of sour cream and salsa over the toppings on each tortilla.
7. Carefully fold in the sides of each tortilla and then roll them up tightly to form a wrap.
8. Place the wraps seam-side down on a serving platter.
9. Optionally, warm the wraps in the skillet for a few minutes to melt the cheese and enhance the flavors.
10. Serve the Witches' Whirlwind Wraps with additional salsa and sour cream on the side for dipping.

Nutrition Information (per serving):
(Note: Nutritional values are approximate and may vary based on specific ingredients and serving sizes.)
- Calories: 450
- Total Fat: 15g
- Saturated Fat: 7g
- Cholesterol: 80mg
- Sodium: 700mg
- Total Carbohydrates: 45g
- Dietary Fiber: 7g
- Sugars: 3g
- Protein: 35g

Delight in the mystical flavors of these Witches' Whirlwind Wraps and make mealtime an adventure worthy of Mystery Inc.!

63. Goblin Gingersnap Cookies

Step into the spooky world of Scooby-Doo with these Goblin Gingersnap Cookies that are sure to satisfy your sweet tooth while keeping an eye out for any mystery-solving canine companions. Inspired by the mischievous ghouls and ghosts the Mystery Inc. gang encounters, these cookies are a delightful blend of warm spices and sweetness. Bake up a batch for your next Scooby-Doo marathon and let the mystery-solving begin!

Serving: Makes approximately 24 cookies
Preparation Time: 15 minutes
Ready Time: 45 minutes

Ingredients:
- 2 1/4 cups all-purpose flour
- 1 teaspoon baking soda
- 1/2 teaspoon salt
- 2 teaspoons ground ginger
- 1 teaspoon ground cinnamon
- 1/2 teaspoon ground cloves
- 3/4 cup unsalted butter, softened
- 1 cup granulated sugar
- 1 large egg
- 1/4 cup molasses
- 1 teaspoon vanilla extract
- Additional granulated sugar for rolling

Instructions:
1. Preheat your oven to 350°F (175°C) and line two baking sheets with parchment paper.
2. In a medium bowl, whisk together the flour, baking soda, salt, ginger, cinnamon, and cloves until well combined. Set aside.
3. In a large bowl or mixer, cream together the softened butter and 1 cup of granulated sugar until light and fluffy.

4. Add the egg to the butter-sugar mixture, beating well after each addition. Then, mix in the molasses and vanilla extract until the batter is smooth.

5. Gradually add the dry ingredients to the wet ingredients, mixing until just combined. Be careful not to overmix.

6. Place additional granulated sugar in a shallow bowl. Scoop out tablespoon-sized portions of cookie dough and roll them into balls. Roll each ball in the sugar until coated, then place them on the prepared baking sheets, leaving enough space between each.

7. Bake in the preheated oven for 10-12 minutes or until the edges are set and the tops are cracked. The cookies will continue to firm up as they cool.

8. Allow the cookies to cool on the baking sheets for 5 minutes before transferring them to a wire rack to cool completely.

Nutrition Information:
Note: Nutrition information is per serving (1 cookie)
- Calories: 120
- Total Fat: 6g
- Saturated Fat: 4g
- Cholesterol: 20mg
- Sodium: 90mg
- Total Carbohydrates: 16g
- Dietary Fiber: 0.5g
- Sugars: 9g
- Protein: 1g

These Goblin Gingersnap Cookies are the perfect treat to enjoy while unmasking mysteries with Scooby-Doo and the gang. So, grab a cookie, settle in, and get ready for a sweet adventure!

64. Ectoplasmic Energy Bars

Step into the mystical world of Scooby-Doo with these Ectoplasmic Energy Bars! Inspired by the ghostly encounters and mysterious adventures of Scooby and the gang, these energy bars are packed with wholesome ingredients to give you the energy you need to solve any spooky mystery.

Serving: Makes 12 bars
Preparation Time: 15 minutes
Ready Time: 2 hours (includes chilling time)

Ingredients:
- 1 cup old-fashioned oats
- 1/2 cup almond butter
- 1/4 cup honey
- 1/4 cup dried cranberries
- 1/4 cup chopped nuts (such as almonds or walnuts)
- 1/4 cup shredded coconut
- 1/4 cup mini chocolate chips
- 1 teaspoon vanilla extract
- 1/2 teaspoon ground cinnamon
- Pinch of salt
- Green food coloring

Instructions:
1. In a large mixing bowl, combine the old-fashioned oats, almond butter, honey, dried cranberries, chopped nuts, shredded coconut, mini chocolate chips, vanilla extract, ground cinnamon, and a pinch of salt.
2. Mix the ingredients together until well combined. The mixture should be sticky and hold together when pressed.
3. Add a few drops of green food coloring to achieve the ectoplasmic green hue. Stir until the color is evenly distributed throughout the mixture.
4. Line a square baking dish with parchment paper, leaving some overhang on the sides for easy removal.
5. Transfer the mixture to the lined baking dish, pressing it down firmly and evenly.
6. Place the dish in the refrigerator and let it chill for at least 2 hours, or until the bars are firm.
7. Once chilled, use the parchment paper overhang to lift the bars out of the dish. Place them on a cutting board and cut into 12 bars.
8. Store the Ectoplasmic Energy Bars in an airtight container in the refrigerator for optimal freshness.

Nutrition Information:
(Per serving - 1 bar)
- Calories: 180

- Total Fat: 10g
- Saturated Fat: 3g
- Trans Fat: 0g
- Cholesterol: 0mg
- Sodium: 30mg
- Total Carbohydrates: 20g
- Dietary Fiber: 3g
- Sugars: 10g
- Protein: 4g

Unleash the supernatural energy within these Ectoplasmic Energy Bars and embark on your own adventurous journey – just like Scooby-Doo and the Mystery Inc. gang!

65. Spectral Strawberry Shortcake

Step into the whimsical world of mystery-solving with this delightful treat inspired by Scooby-Doo and the gang. The Spectral Strawberry Shortcake is a sweet and ghostly twist on the classic dessert, perfect for satisfying your sweet tooth after a thrilling adventure. The vibrant red strawberries and fluffy layers will have you saying, "Zoinks! That's delicious!"

Serving: Makes 8 servings
Preparation Time: 20 minutes
Ready Time: 2 hours (including chilling time)

Ingredients:
- 2 cups fresh strawberries, hulled and sliced
- 1/2 cup granulated sugar
- 2 tablespoons strawberry jam
- 2 cups heavy cream
- 1/4 cup powdered sugar
- 1 teaspoon vanilla extract
- 1 package (10 ounces) store-bought shortcakes or homemade if preferred
- Ghost-shaped cookie cutters (optional, for decoration)

Instructions:

1. Prepare the Strawberries:
- In a bowl, combine the sliced strawberries, granulated sugar, and strawberry jam. Toss gently to coat the strawberries in the sugar and jam mixture. Set aside to allow the strawberries to release their juices.

2. Whip the Cream:
- In a separate bowl, whip the heavy cream until soft peaks form. Add the powdered sugar and vanilla extract, and continue to whip until stiff peaks form. Be careful not to over-whip.

3. Assemble the Shortcakes:
- Slice the shortcakes in half horizontally. Place the bottom halves on a serving platter.
- Spoon a generous layer of the sugared strawberries onto the shortcake bottoms.
- Top with a dollop of whipped cream.
- Place the shortcake tops over the whipped cream.

4. Decorate (Optional):
- If desired, use ghost-shaped cookie cutters to cut out ghost shapes from additional shortcakes or white fondant. Place these ghost shapes on top of the whipped cream for a spooky touch.

5. Chill:
- Refrigerate the assembled shortcakes for at least 1-2 hours to allow the flavors to meld and the dessert to chill.

6. Serve:
- Serve the Spectral Strawberry Shortcake chilled, and enjoy this ghostly delight inspired by Scooby-Doo!

Nutrition Information:
(Per Serving)
- Calories: 320
- Total Fat: 20g
- Saturated Fat: 12g
- Cholesterol: 70mg
- Sodium: 150mg
- Total Carbohydrates: 34g
- Dietary Fiber: 2g
- Sugars: 18g
- Protein: 3g

Savor the magic of Scooby-Doo with every delicious bite of this Spectral Strawberry Shortcake. It's a treat that even the Mystery Inc. gang would be eager to enjoy after unmasking another spooky villain!

66. Ghostly Garlic Bread

Welcome to the spooky world of Scooby-Doo, where mysteries unfold and appetites grow! Our "Ghostly Garlic Bread" recipe is inspired by the eerie encounters of Scooby-Doo and the gang. This garlic bread is not only delicious but also a fun and thematic addition to your Scooby-Doo-inspired feast. Whip it up for your next gathering and watch as everyone solves the mystery of the disappearing garlic flavor!

Serving: Makes approximately 8 servings.
Preparation Time: 15 minutes
Ready Time: 20 minutes

Ingredients:
- 1 loaf of French bread
- 1/2 cup unsalted butter, softened
- 4 cloves garlic, minced
- 2 tablespoons fresh parsley, finely chopped
- 1/2 teaspoon onion powder
- 1/4 teaspoon salt
- 1/4 teaspoon black pepper
- 1 cup shredded mozzarella cheese
- Optional: Ghost-shaped cookie cutter

Instructions:
1. Preheat your oven to 375°F (190°C).
2. Slice the French bread in half lengthwise, creating two long pieces. If you have a ghost-shaped cookie cutter, you can use it to cut ghost shapes out of each bread half. Set aside the ghost-shaped pieces.
3. In a small bowl, combine the softened butter, minced garlic, chopped parsley, onion powder, salt, and black pepper. Mix until well combined.
4. Spread the garlic butter mixture evenly over the cut sides of the French bread.
5. If you have ghost-shaped pieces, place them on a baking sheet lined with parchment paper.
6. Sprinkle the shredded mozzarella cheese over the garlic butter-covered bread.

7. Place the bread (and ghost-shaped pieces if using) in the preheated oven and bake for about 12-15 minutes or until the cheese is melted and bubbly, and the edges of the bread are golden brown.
8. If you made ghost-shaped pieces, remove them from the oven a couple of minutes earlier to preserve their shape.
9. Once done, let the garlic bread cool for a few minutes before slicing. Serve warm and watch as your guests devour this ghostly delight!

Nutrition Information:
Note: Nutrition information is approximate and may vary based on specific ingredients used.
- Serving Size: 1 slice (without ghost-shaped pieces)
- Calories: 250
- Total Fat: 14g
- Saturated Fat: 8g
- Trans Fat: 0g
- Cholesterol: 35mg
- Sodium: 380mg
- Total Carbohydrates: 25g
- Dietary Fiber: 1g
- Sugars: 1g
- Protein: 7g

Enjoy your Ghostly Garlic Bread and may your Scooby-Doo-inspired feast be filled with flavor and fun!

67. Bat Berry Smoothie Bowl

Indulge in the mysterious and delightful world of Scooby-Doo with our Bat Berry Smoothie Bowl—a bewitching treat that combines the excitement of solving mysteries with the goodness of a wholesome and delicious breakfast. Packed with vibrant flavors and a dash of fun, this smoothie bowl is sure to transport you to the spooky yet charming universe of everyone's favorite Great Dane and his gang. So, grab your magnifying glass and get ready to uncover the secret behind the delectable Bat Berry Smoothie Bowl!

Serving: 2 servings
Preparation Time: 15 minutes

Ready Time: 15 minutes

Ingredients:
- 2 frozen bananas
- 1 cup mixed berries (blueberries, blackberries, and raspberries)
- 1/2 cup Greek yogurt
- 1/4 cup almond milk
- 2 tablespoons chia seeds
- 1 tablespoon honey
- 1 teaspoon activated charcoal powder (for the bat effect)
- Toppings: sliced strawberries, granola, shredded coconut, and mint leaves

Instructions:
1. Prepare the Base:
- In a blender, combine the frozen bananas, mixed berries, Greek yogurt, almond milk, chia seeds, honey, and activated charcoal powder.
- Blend until smooth and creamy, adjusting the consistency with more almond milk if needed.
2. Create the Bat Effect:
- Pour the smoothie into two bowls, creating a circular shape for the bat's body.
- Use a toothpick or the back of a spoon to draw wings on the smoothie surface, giving it a bat-like appearance.
3. Add Toppings:
- Place sliced strawberries strategically as eyes and granola as the bat's wings to enhance the spooky yet adorable effect.
- Sprinkle shredded coconut around the smoothie bowl to create a misty atmosphere.
4. Garnish:
- Finish by garnishing with mint leaves to add a burst of freshness.
5. Serve:
- Serve immediately and enjoy the Bat Berry Smoothie Bowl as a whimsical and nutritious breakfast.

Nutrition Information:
Per Serving
- Calories: 250
- Protein: 8g
- Carbohydrates: 50g

- Fiber: 10g
- Sugar: 30g
- Fat: 4g
- Saturated Fat: 1g
- Cholesterol: 5mg
- Sodium: 40mg
- Potassium: 600mg
- Vitamin C: 30%
- Iron: 2%

68. Enchanted Egg Salad

Welcome to the delightful world of Scooby-Doo-inspired cuisine! The Enchanted Egg Salad captures the essence of mystery-solving picnics and combines it with the charm of this beloved classic. It's a dish that's not only easy to prepare but also packs a flavorful punch that will leave everyone craving more. Let's dive into this bewitching recipe!

Serving: Serves 4
Preparation Time: 15 minutes
Ready Time: 15 minutes

Ingredients:
- 6 hard-boiled eggs, chopped
- 1/4 cup mayonnaise
- 2 tablespoons Dijon mustard
- 1/4 cup finely chopped red onion
- 1/4 cup finely chopped celery
- 2 tablespoons finely chopped fresh parsley
- Salt and pepper to taste
- 1/2 teaspoon paprika (for garnish)
- Optional: Dash of hot sauce for a spicy twist

Instructions:
1. Prepare the Eggs: Start by boiling the eggs until they are hard-boiled. Once cooled, peel and chop them into small pieces.

2. Mix the Base: In a mixing bowl, combine the chopped eggs, mayonnaise, Dijon mustard, red onion, celery, and fresh parsley. Mix well until all ingredients are evenly incorporated.

3. Season to Perfection: Season the egg salad with salt and pepper according to your taste. For a bit of extra kick, add a dash of hot sauce if desired.

4. Chill and Serve: Cover the bowl and refrigerate the enchanted egg salad for about 15 minutes to let the flavors meld together. When ready to serve, sprinkle paprika on top for a vibrant finish.

5. Enjoy the Magic: Serve the enchanted egg salad on a bed of lettuce, between slices of bread for sandwiches, or as a topping for crackers. It's a bewitching treat perfect for any Scooby-Doo-themed gathering!

Nutrition Information (per serving):
- Calories: 215
- Total Fat: 17g
- Saturated Fat: 4g
- Cholesterol: 283mg
- Sodium: 315mg
- Total Carbohydrate: 3g
- Dietary Fiber: 1g
- Sugars: 2g
- Protein: 11g

This Enchanted Egg Salad is a quick, flavorful addition to any mealtime adventure. It's a dish that Scooby-Doo and the gang would eagerly devour after unraveling a mysterious caper!

69. Jack-O'-Lantern Jalapeño Poppers

Scooby-Doo and his gang often found themselves in spooky situations, especially around Halloween. These Jack-O'-Lantern Jalapeño Poppers pay homage to the thrilling and playful adventures they embarked upon. These fiery bites will add a zing to any gathering, perfect for a spooky-themed party or simply for those who love a bit of heat in their snacks.

Serving: Makes 20 poppers
Preparation time: 20 minutes
Ready time: 40 minutes

Ingredients:
- 10 large jalapeño peppers
- 8 ounces cream cheese, softened
- 1 cup shredded cheddar cheese
- 1 teaspoon garlic powder
- 1 teaspoon onion powder
- 1/2 teaspoon smoked paprika
- Salt and pepper to taste
- Green food coloring (optional)
- Cooking spray
- Black olives (optional, for decoration)

Instructions:
1. Preheat the oven to 375°F (190°C) and line a baking sheet with parchment paper.
2. Prepare the jalapeños: Cut the jalapeños in half lengthwise and scoop out the seeds and membranes. If you want a milder flavor, rinse the jalapeño halves under cold water. Dry them thoroughly with paper towels.
3. Make the filling: In a mixing bowl, combine the softened cream cheese, shredded cheddar cheese, garlic powder, onion powder, smoked paprika, salt, and pepper. Mix until well combined. If desired, add a few drops of green food coloring to achieve a vibrant green color resembling a Jack-O'-Lantern.
4. Fill the jalapeños: Spoon the cheese mixture into each jalapeño half, filling them generously.
5. Shape the Jack-O'-Lantern faces: Using a small paring knife, carefully carve faces onto the filled jalapeños to resemble Jack-O'-Lanterns. You can create spooky or silly faces—let your imagination run wild! Optionally, use small pieces of black olives to create eyes, noses, or mouths for added detail.
6. Bake the poppers: Place the filled jalapeños on the prepared baking sheet and lightly spray them with cooking spray. Bake in the preheated oven for 20-25 minutes, or until the peppers are tender and the cheese is melted and slightly golden on top.
7. Serve: Allow the poppers to cool for a few minutes before serving. These Jack-O'-Lantern Jalapeño Poppers are best enjoyed warm and make a delightful, spicy treat for any Scooby-Doo-themed gathering.

Nutrition Information (per serving, based on 2 poppers):
- Calories: 110
- Total Fat: 9g
- Saturated Fat: 5g
- Cholesterol: 25mg
- Sodium: 180mg
- Total Carbohydrate: 3g
- Dietary Fiber: 1g
- Sugars: 1g
- Protein: 4g

Enjoy these spooky and delicious Jack-O'-Lantern Jalapeño Poppers straight from the oven or alongside your favorite Scooby-Doo episodes for a memorable snacking experience!

70. Devilishly Dark Chocolate Fondue

Unraveling mysteries with Scooby-Doo and his gang always calls for a tantalizing treat! Dive into the wickedly indulgent world of "Devilishly Dark Chocolate Fondue" - a concoction sure to lure even the most mysterious taste buds. This easy-to-make, sinfully rich fondue is perfect for gatherings or cozy nights in while unmasking those puzzling culinary cravings!

Serving: 4-6 people
Preparation time: 10 minutes
Ready time: 15 minutes

Ingredients:
- 12 ounces dark chocolate (70% cocoa or higher), finely chopped
- 1 cup heavy cream
- 1 teaspoon pure vanilla extract
- Assorted dippables (strawberries, bananas, marshmallows, pretzels, pound cake, etc.)

Instructions:
1. Prepare the Ingredients: Chop the dark chocolate finely to ensure quick and even melting. Wash and pat dry the fruits you plan to use as dippables.

2. Heat the Cream: In a saucepan over medium heat, warm the heavy cream until it simmers. Be cautious not to bring it to a boil.
3. Combine Chocolate and Cream: Remove the cream from heat and pour it over the chopped dark chocolate in a heatproof bowl. Let it sit for a minute to allow the chocolate to soften.
4. Stir and Blend: Gently stir the chocolate and cream mixture until it becomes smooth and glossy. Add vanilla extract and stir again to incorporate.
5. Set Up the Fondue: Transfer the chocolate mixture to a fondue pot or a heatproof bowl that can sit over a candle or fondue burner to keep it warm and melted.
6. Dip and Enjoy: Arrange your assorted dippables on a platter or individual plates around the fondue pot. Use skewers or fondue forks to dip the goodies into the luscious dark chocolate fondue.
7. Indulge! Dive into the velvety goodness and savor each devilishly delightful bite!

Nutrition Information (per serving):
- Calories: Approximately 300
- Fat: 20g
- Saturated Fat: 12g
- Carbohydrates: 25g
- Sugar: 15g
- Protein: 3g

Adjust serving sizes and ingredients for variations in nutritional content. This delectable Devilishly Dark Chocolate Fondue is an irresistible companion for Scooby-Doo-inspired gatherings, providing a sweet treat that even the most discerning detectives won't be able to resist!

71. Zombie Zoodle Salad

Step into the mysterious world of Scooby-Doo and his gang with the "Zombie Zoodle Salad" – a dish inspired by the spine-chilling adventures and intriguing mysteries solved by our favorite crime-solving crew. This zesty and colorful salad captures the essence of Scooby-Doo's exciting escapades and is perfect for those who love a combination of fresh flavors and a hint of spookiness. So, gather your gang, and get ready to solve the mystery of hunger with this deliciously eerie dish!

Serving: 4 servings
Preparation Time: 15 minutes
Ready Time: 20 minutes

Ingredients:
- 2 medium zucchinis, spiralized into zoodles
- 1 cup cherry tomatoes, halved
- 1 cup cucumber, thinly sliced
- 1/2 cup black olives, sliced
- 1/4 cup red onion, finely chopped
- 1/2 cup feta cheese, crumbled
- 1/4 cup fresh parsley, chopped

Dressing:
- 3 tablespoons olive oil
- 2 tablespoons red wine vinegar
- 1 teaspoon Dijon mustard
- 1 clove garlic, minced
- Salt and pepper to taste

Instructions:
1. In a large bowl, combine the zoodles, cherry tomatoes, cucumber, black olives, red onion, feta cheese, and fresh parsley.
2. In a separate small bowl, whisk together the olive oil, red wine vinegar, Dijon mustard, minced garlic, salt, and pepper to create the dressing.
3. Pour the dressing over the salad and toss gently until all ingredients are well coated.
4. Allow the salad to marinate for at least 5 minutes to let the flavors meld together.
5. Serve the Zombie Zoodle Salad in individual bowls or on a platter, and garnish with extra feta cheese and parsley if desired.
6. Enjoy this refreshing and mysterious salad as a standalone meal or as a side dish to complement your Scooby-Doo-themed feast!

Nutrition Information:
(Per Serving)
- Calories: 180
- Total Fat: 14g
- Saturated Fat: 4g
- Trans Fat: 0g

- Cholesterol: 15mg
- Sodium: 300mg
- Total Carbohydrates: 10g
- Dietary Fiber: 3g
- Sugars: 5g
- Protein: 5g

Note: Nutrition information is approximate and may vary based on specific ingredients used.

72. Mysterious Maple Glazed Carrots

Step into the world of mystery and indulgence with our "Mysterious Maple Glazed Carrots" inspired by the iconic Scooby-Doo and his gang's adventures. These sweet and savory glazed carrots are a delightful addition to any meal, and the touch of maple syrup adds a mysterious twist that will leave your taste buds intrigued and satisfied.

Serving: 4 servings
Preparation Time: 15 minutes
Ready Time: 35 minutes

Ingredients:
- 1 pound (about 450g) baby carrots, washed and peeled
- 2 tablespoons olive oil
- 2 tablespoons maple syrup
- 1 tablespoon balsamic vinegar
- 1 teaspoon Dijon mustard
- 1/2 teaspoon salt
- 1/4 teaspoon black pepper
- 1/4 teaspoon garlic powder
- 1/4 teaspoon smoked paprika
- Fresh parsley, chopped (for garnish)

Instructions:
1. Preheat the Oven: Preheat your oven to 400°F (200°C).
2. Prepare the Carrots: Place the baby carrots on a baking sheet, ensuring they are spread out evenly.

3. Make the Glaze: In a small bowl, whisk together the olive oil, maple syrup, balsamic vinegar, Dijon mustard, salt, black pepper, garlic powder, and smoked paprika until well combined.
4. Coat the Carrots: Pour the glaze over the baby carrots and toss them gently to ensure they are evenly coated.
5. Roast in the Oven: Place the baking sheet in the preheated oven and roast the carrots for about 20-25 minutes or until they are tender and caramelized, turning them halfway through.
6. Garnish and Serve: Remove the carrots from the oven, and garnish with freshly chopped parsley for a burst of freshness.
7. Serve Warm: These Mysterious Maple Glazed Carrots are best served warm. Enjoy them as a side dish to your favorite main course.

Nutrition Information:
(Per Serving)
- Calories: 150
- Total Fat: 7g
- Saturated Fat: 1g
- Cholesterol: 0mg
- Sodium: 380mg
- Total Carbohydrates: 21g
- Dietary Fiber: 4g
- Sugars: 12g
- Protein: 1g

Unravel the mystery of flavor with these delectable glazed carrots, perfect for bringing a touch of intrigue to your dining table!

73. Hauntingly Healthy Hummus

Get ready to embark on a spooky and savory culinary adventure with our "Hauntingly Healthy Hummus" inspired by the mystery-solving gang of Scooby-Doo! Packed with wholesome ingredients and a dash of mystery, this hummus is perfect for any gathering of ghost hunters or midnight snackers. Uncover the secret to a nutritious and delicious dip that will have you saying, "Scooby-Dooby-Doo, where are you?" in delight.

Serving: Makes approximately 2 cups of Hauntingly Healthy Hummus.
Preparation Time: 15 minutes

Ready Time: 15 minutes

Ingredients:
- 1 can (15 ounces) chickpeas, drained and rinsed
- 1/3 cup tahini
- 2 tablespoons extra-virgin olive oil, plus extra for drizzling
- 1 clove garlic, minced
- 1 teaspoon ground cumin
- 1/2 teaspoon smoked paprika
- Juice of 1 lemon
- 1/2 teaspoon salt, or to taste
- 2-3 tablespoons water (as needed for desired consistency)
- Optional toppings: chopped fresh parsley, black sesame seeds, or a sprinkle of additional smoked paprika

Instructions:
1. In a food processor, combine the chickpeas, tahini, olive oil, minced garlic, cumin, smoked paprika, lemon juice, and salt.
2. Blend the ingredients until smooth, stopping occasionally to scrape down the sides of the food processor with a spatula.
3. If the hummus is too thick, add water, one tablespoon at a time, until you reach your desired consistency.
4. Taste the hummus and adjust the seasoning, adding more salt or lemon juice as needed.
5. Once the hummus is smooth and flavorful, transfer it to a serving bowl.
6. Drizzle with extra olive oil and sprinkle with optional toppings such as chopped fresh parsley, black sesame seeds, or a touch of smoked paprika.
7. Serve your Hauntingly Healthy Hummus with a variety of dippable delights, such as carrot sticks, cucumber slices, or pita bread.

Nutrition Information:
Note: Nutrition information is approximate and may vary based on specific ingredients used and serving sizes.
- Serving Size: 2 tablespoons
- Calories: 70
- Total Fat: 4g
- Saturated Fat: 0.5g
- Cholesterol: 0mg

- Sodium: 80mg
- Total Carbohydrates: 7g
- Dietary Fiber: 2g
- Sugars: 0g
- Protein: 2.5g

Enjoy this Hauntingly Healthy Hummus as a satisfying and mysterious snack that will leave you energized for your next mystery-solving adventure!

74. Poltergeist Pumpkin Pie

Embark on a spooky culinary adventure with our "Poltergeist Pumpkin Pie," inspired by the mysterious and thrilling world of Scooby-Doo. This delectable dessert is not only a treat for your taste buds but also a nod to the ghostly encounters and thrilling investigations that Scooby-Doo and the gang have undertaken. Get ready to enjoy a slice of deliciousness with a hint of mystery!

Serving: Makes one 9-inch pie, serving 8.
Preparation Time: 20 minutes
Ready Time: 4 hours (including chilling time)

Ingredients:
- 1 ½ cups graham cracker crumbs
- 1/3 cup melted butter
- 1/4 cup granulated sugar
- 1 can (15 ounces) pumpkin puree
- 3 large eggs
- 1 cup brown sugar, packed
- 1 teaspoon ground cinnamon
- 1/2 teaspoon ground ginger
- 1/4 teaspoon ground cloves
- 1/2 teaspoon salt
- 1 1/2 cups evaporated milk
- Whipped cream, for serving (optional)

Instructions:
1. Preheat your oven to 350°F (175°C).

2. In a medium-sized bowl, combine the graham cracker crumbs, melted butter, and granulated sugar. Press the mixture into the bottom of a 9-inch pie dish to form the crust. Bake in the preheated oven for 8-10 minutes or until set. Allow it to cool while preparing the filling.
3. In a large mixing bowl, whisk together the pumpkin puree, eggs, brown sugar, cinnamon, ginger, cloves, and salt until well combined.
4. Gradually add the evaporated milk to the pumpkin mixture, stirring continuously until smooth.
5. Pour the pumpkin filling into the prepared crust. Bake in the preheated oven for 40-45 minutes or until the center is set.
6. Allow the pie to cool completely on a wire rack, then refrigerate for at least 3 hours or until chilled.
7. Serve chilled, optionally topped with whipped cream for an extra indulgence.

Nutrition Information:
Note: Nutrition values are approximate and may vary based on specific ingredients and serving sizes.
- Calories: 320 per serving
- Total Fat: 14g
- Saturated Fat: 7g
- Cholesterol: 85mg
- Sodium: 310mg
- Total Carbohydrates: 45g
- Dietary Fiber: 2g
- Sugars: 34g
- Protein: 6g

Unleash your inner detective as you savor the hauntingly delicious "Poltergeist Pumpkin Pie" – a perfect addition to your Scooby-Doo-inspired culinary collection!

75. Abominable Avocado Toast

Embark on a culinary adventure inspired by the mystery-solving gang from Scooby-Doo with our "Abominable Avocado Toast." This delectable twist on a classic dish combines creamy avocado with a medley of savory flavors, creating a satisfying and wholesome treat that even Scooby and Shaggy would approve of. Unmask the secret to a delightful meal that's perfect for breakfast, brunch, or anytime you're craving a Scooby snack.

Serving: Makes 2 servings
Preparation Time: 15 minutes
Ready Time: 15 minutes

Ingredients:
- 2 ripe avocados
- 4 slices of your favorite bread (sourdough or whole grain work well)
- 1 clove garlic, peeled
- 2 tablespoons olive oil
- Salt and pepper to taste
- 1 cup cherry tomatoes, halved
- 1/4 cup feta cheese, crumbled
- 2 tablespoons fresh cilantro, chopped
- Red pepper flakes (optional, for spice)

Instructions:
1. Prepare the Avocado Smash:
- Cut the avocados in half, remove the pits, and scoop the flesh into a bowl.
- Mash the avocados with a fork until smooth but still slightly chunky.
- Add salt and pepper to taste, and mix well.
2. Toast the Bread:
- Toast the slices of bread to your desired level of crispiness.
3. Rub with Garlic:
- While the bread is still warm, rub each slice with the peeled garlic clove for a subtle garlic flavor.
4. Assemble the Abominable Avocado Toast:
- Spread the mashed avocado evenly onto each slice of toasted bread.
5. Top with Toppings:
- Scatter halved cherry tomatoes, crumbled feta cheese, and chopped cilantro over the avocado-covered toast.
6. Drizzle with Olive Oil:
- Finish off by drizzling olive oil over each toast for an extra layer of richness.
7. Optional Spice:
- If you like a bit of heat, sprinkle red pepper flakes over the top.
8. Serve and Enjoy:

- Serve the Abominable Avocado Toast immediately, and savor the irresistible combination of creamy avocado, savory toppings, and crunchy bread.

Nutrition Information:
(Per Serving)
- Calories: 350
- Total Fat: 25g
- Saturated Fat: 5g
- Trans Fat: 0g
- Cholesterol: 10mg
- Sodium: 400mg
- Total Carbohydrates: 30g
- Dietary Fiber: 12g
- Sugars: 4g
- Protein: 8g

Unleash your inner detective and relish the flavors of the "Abominable Avocado Toast" – a culinary mystery solved!

76. Batty Blueberry Muffins

Join Scooby-Doo and the gang on another culinary adventure with these "Batty Blueberry Muffins." Inspired by the mystery-solving antics of our favorite canine detective, these muffins are sure to be a hit at breakfast or as a snack. Packed with plump blueberries and a hint of sweetness, they're perfect for satisfying those mysterious cravings!

Serving: Makes 12 muffins
Preparation Time: 15 minutes
Ready Time: 35 minutes

Ingredients:
- 2 cups all-purpose flour
- 1/2 cup granulated sugar
- 1/4 cup brown sugar, packed
- 2 teaspoons baking powder
- 1/2 teaspoon baking soda
- 1/4 teaspoon salt

- 1 cup fresh or frozen blueberries
- 1 cup milk
- 1/2 cup unsalted butter, melted
- 2 large eggs
- 1 teaspoon vanilla extract
- 1 tablespoon lemon zest (optional, for a citrusy twist)

Instructions:
1. Preheat your oven to 375°F (190°C). Line a muffin tin with paper liners or grease the cups.
2. In a large bowl, whisk together the flour, granulated sugar, brown sugar, baking powder, baking soda, and salt.
3. In a separate bowl, combine the melted butter, milk, eggs, and vanilla extract. Mix well.
4. Pour the wet ingredients into the dry ingredients and stir until just combined. Be careful not to overmix; a few lumps are okay.
5. Gently fold in the blueberries and lemon zest, if using.
6. Spoon the batter into the muffin cups, filling each about two-thirds full.
7. Bake for 18-20 minutes or until a toothpick inserted into the center of a muffin comes out clean.
8. Allow the muffins to cool in the tin for 5 minutes, then transfer them to a wire rack to cool completely.

Nutrition Information:
(Per serving - 1 muffin)
- Calories: 200
- Total Fat: 8g
- Saturated Fat: 5g
- Trans Fat: 0g
- Cholesterol: 45mg
- Sodium: 180mg
- Total Carbohydrates: 29g
- Dietary Fiber: 1g
- Sugars: 12g
- Protein: 4g

Note: Nutrition information is approximate and may vary based on specific ingredients used.

77. Mummy Mango Salsa

Get ready for a thrilling culinary adventure with our "Mummy Mango Salsa," inspired by the mysterious and delightful world of Scooby-Doo. This zesty salsa is a perfect blend of sweet and spicy, capturing the essence of Scooby and the gang's escapades. Whether you're solving mysteries or just enjoying a snack, this Mummy Mango Salsa is sure to tantalize your taste buds!

Serving: Ideal as a vibrant topping for tacos, nachos, or grilled chicken, our Mummy Mango Salsa serves 4.
Preparation Time: 15 minutes
Ready Time: 15 minutes

Ingredients:
- 2 ripe mangoes, diced
- 1 cup cherry tomatoes, quartered
- 1/2 red onion, finely diced
- 1 jalapeño, seeds removed and finely chopped
- 1/4 cup fresh cilantro, chopped
- Juice of 2 limes
- 1 tablespoon honey
- 1/2 teaspoon ground cumin
- Salt and pepper to taste

Instructions:
1. In a large mixing bowl, combine the diced mangoes, quartered cherry tomatoes, finely diced red onion, chopped jalapeño, and fresh cilantro.
2. In a separate small bowl, whisk together the lime juice, honey, ground cumin, salt, and pepper to create the dressing.
3. Pour the dressing over the mango mixture and gently toss until well combined. Adjust the seasoning to taste.
4. Allow the Mummy Mango Salsa to sit for at least 10 minutes to let the flavors meld together.
5. Serve the salsa on top of tacos, nachos, or alongside grilled chicken for a deliciously Scooby-Doo inspired treat.

Nutrition Information:
(Per Serving)
- Calories: 120

- Total Fat: 0.5g
- Cholesterol: 0mg
- Sodium: 5mg
- Total Carbohydrates: 30g
- Dietary Fiber: 3g
- Sugars: 23g
- Protein: 2g

Embark on a culinary journey with this Mummy Mango Salsa, a tribute to the timeless adventures of Scooby-Doo and friends. Enjoy the taste of mystery and fun in every bite!

78. Wicked Walnut Trail Mix

Indulge your taste buds in a mysterious medley of flavors with our "Wicked Walnut Trail Mix," inspired by the adventurous spirit of Scooby-Doo and the gang. Packed with the goodness of crunchy walnuts, sweet dried fruits, and a touch of spice, this trail mix is the perfect snack for your next sleuthing expedition. Whether you're unmasking villains or satisfying your snack cravings, this wickedly delicious mix is sure to keep you energized and ready for the next clue.

Serving: Makes approximately 8 servings.
Preparation Time: 15 minutes.
Ready Time: 15 minutes.

Ingredients:
- 1 cup walnuts, halved
- 1 cup almonds, whole
- 1 cup dried cranberries
- 1 cup dried mango, diced
- 1 cup dark chocolate chunks
- 1/2 cup pumpkin seeds
- 1/2 cup honey
- 2 tablespoons olive oil
- 1 teaspoon ground cinnamon
- 1/2 teaspoon cayenne pepper (adjust to taste)
- 1/2 teaspoon sea salt

Instructions:
1. Preheat and Toast:
Preheat your oven to 325°F (163°C). Place the walnuts, almonds, and pumpkin seeds on a baking sheet and toast them in the oven for about 8-10 minutes or until they become fragrant and lightly golden. Make sure to stir occasionally for even toasting.
2. Mix and Mingle:
In a large bowl, combine the toasted walnuts, almonds, pumpkin seeds, dried cranberries, dried mango, and dark chocolate chunks. Mix well to ensure an even distribution of ingredients.
3. Sweet and Spicy Coating:
In a small saucepan over low heat, combine the honey, olive oil, ground cinnamon, cayenne pepper, and sea salt. Stir until the mixture is well combined and heated through.
4. Drizzle and Toss:
Drizzle the sweet and spicy mixture over the nut and fruit mixture. Use a spatula or wooden spoon to gently toss everything together, ensuring all components are evenly coated.
5. Cool and Crisp:
Allow the trail mix to cool completely. This will help the honey mixture to set and create a delightful crunchy texture.
6. Serve and Share:
Once cooled, your Wicked Walnut Trail Mix is ready to serve. Pack it into individual portions for on-the-go snacks or share a bowlful with friends during your next Scooby-Doo marathon.

Nutrition Information:
Note: Nutritional values are approximate and may vary based on specific ingredients used.
- Serving Size: 1/2 cup
- Calories: 250
- Total Fat: 15g
- Saturated Fat: 4g
- Cholesterol: 0mg
- Sodium: 60mg
- Total Carbohydrates: 28g
- Dietary Fiber: 4g
- Sugars: 18g
- Protein: 5g

Unleash your inner detective with this Wicked Walnut Trail Mix, a snack that's both satisfying and filled with the spirit of mystery-solving adventures!

79. Mocha Monster Brownie Bites

Get ready to embark on a delicious adventure with our Mocha Monster Brownie Bites, inspired by the iconic Scooby-Doo and his insatiable love for treats! These bite-sized wonders combine the rich flavors of chocolate and coffee, creating a delightful blend that even the Mystery Inc. gang would find irresistible. Perfect for sharing during mystery-solving marathons or satisfying your sweet tooth cravings, these Mocha Monster Brownie Bites are sure to be a hit with kids and adults alike.

Serving: Makes approximately 24 brownie bites
Preparation Time: 15 minutes
Ready Time: 45 minutes

Ingredients:
- 1 cup unsalted butter, melted
- 1 ½ cups granulated sugar
- 3 large eggs
- 1 teaspoon vanilla extract
- 1 cup all-purpose flour
- ½ cup unsweetened cocoa powder
- 1 tablespoon instant coffee granules
- ½ teaspoon baking powder
- ¼ teaspoon salt
- ½ cup chocolate chips
- ½ cup chopped walnuts or pecans (optional)

Instructions:
1. Preheat your oven to 350°F (175°C). Grease a mini muffin tin or line it with paper liners.
2. In a large mixing bowl, whisk together the melted butter and sugar until well combined.
3. Add the eggs one at a time, beating well after each addition. Stir in the vanilla extract.

4. In a separate bowl, sift together the flour, cocoa powder, instant coffee granules, baking powder, and salt.
5. Gradually add the dry ingredients to the wet ingredients, mixing until just combined.
6. Fold in the chocolate chips and chopped nuts (if using) until evenly distributed in the batter.
7. Using a cookie scoop or spoon, fill each mini muffin cup about two-thirds full with the brownie batter.
8. Bake in the preheated oven for 12-15 minutes or until a toothpick inserted into the center comes out with moist crumbs.
9. Allow the brownie bites to cool in the muffin tin for 5 minutes before transferring them to a wire rack to cool completely.
10. Serve and enjoy these Mocha Monster Brownie Bites with a cup of coffee or your favorite Scooby-Doo-inspired beverage!

Nutrition Information:
(Per Brownie Bite)
- Calories: 120
- Total Fat: 8g
- Saturated Fat: 5g
- Cholesterol: 35mg
- Sodium: 40mg
- Total Carbohydrates: 12g
- Dietary Fiber: 1g
- Sugars: 8g
- Protein: 2g

Note: Nutrition information is approximate and may vary based on specific ingredients and portion sizes.

80. Wacky Watercress Wraps

Get ready for a culinary adventure that's straight out of the Mystery Machine! Inspired by Scooby-Doo's love for quirky snacks, these "Wacky Watercress Wraps" are a delightful blend of flavors and textures. Packed with the goodness of watercress and a medley of colorful vegetables, these wraps are perfect for a quick and healthy snack. Join Scooby and the gang in solving mysteries while savoring these scrumptious wraps that are sure to tantalize your taste buds.

Serving: Makes 4 servings
Preparation Time: 15 minutes
Ready Time: 15 minutes

Ingredients:
- 1 bunch of fresh watercress, washed and trimmed
- 4 large whole-grain or spinach tortillas
- 1 cup shredded cooked chicken or tofu for a vegetarian option
- 1 cup cherry tomatoes, halved
- 1 cucumber, julienned
- 1 bell pepper, thinly sliced
- 1 avocado, sliced
- 1/2 cup crumbled feta cheese (optional)
- 1/4 cup hummus or your favorite dressing
- Salt and pepper to taste

Instructions:
1. Lay out the tortillas on a clean surface.
2. Spread a generous layer of hummus or your favorite dressing over each tortilla.
3. Evenly distribute the watercress over the tortillas, leaving space around the edges.
4. Place the shredded chicken or tofu on top of the watercress.
5. Arrange the cherry tomatoes, cucumber, bell pepper, and avocado slices over the chicken or tofu.
6. If using, sprinkle the crumbled feta cheese over the vegetables.
7. Season with salt and pepper to taste.
8. Carefully fold in the sides of each tortilla and then roll them up tightly, creating a wrap.
9. Slice each wrap in half diagonally.
10. Serve immediately and enjoy your Wacky Watercress Wraps with a sense of mystery and adventure!

Nutrition Information:
(Per serving)
- Calories: 350
- Total Fat: 15g
- Saturated Fat: 4g
- Cholesterol: 40mg

- Sodium: 550mg
- Total Carbohydrates: 38g
- Dietary Fiber: 8g
- Sugars: 6g
- Protein: 18g

Note: Nutrition information is approximate and may vary based on specific ingredients and brands used. Adjustments can be made for dietary preferences and restrictions.

81. Goblin Gravy

Embark on a culinary adventure inspired by the mystery-solving gang from Scooby-Doo with our whimsical "Goblin Gravy." This savory concoction is sure to transport you to the spooky and delicious world of Scooby and his friends. Perfect for a cozy night in or a themed gathering, this dish combines rich flavors with a touch of playfulness that will leave you and your guests craving more.

Serving: 4-6 servings
Preparation Time: 15 minutes
Ready Time: 1 hour

Ingredients:
- 1 pound ground beef
- 1 cup diced onions
- 1 cup sliced mushrooms
- 2 cloves garlic, minced
- 1/4 cup all-purpose flour
- 4 cups beef broth
- 1/2 cup tomato sauce
- 1 teaspoon Worcestershire sauce
- 1 teaspoon dried thyme
- 1 teaspoon dried rosemary
- Salt and pepper to taste
- 2 tablespoons olive oil
- Cooked rice or mashed potatoes for serving (optional)

Instructions:

1. In a large skillet, heat olive oil over medium heat. Add onions and garlic, sautéing until softened.
2. Add ground beef to the skillet, breaking it apart with a spatula. Cook until browned.
3. Sprinkle flour over the meat mixture, stirring well to combine. This will create a roux and thicken the gravy.
4. Pour in the beef broth, stirring continuously to avoid lumps. Add mushrooms, tomato sauce, Worcestershire sauce, thyme, rosemary, salt, and pepper. Bring the mixture to a simmer.
5. Reduce the heat to low, cover, and let it simmer for about 45 minutes, allowing the flavors to meld.
6. Taste and adjust seasoning if needed. If the gravy is too thick, you can add more beef broth until it reaches your desired consistency.
7. Serve the Goblin Gravy over cooked rice or mashed potatoes, if desired.

Nutrition Information:
(Per serving, based on 4 servings)
- Calories: 380
- Protein: 22g
- Fat: 25g
- Carbohydrates: 18g
- Fiber: 2g
- Sugar: 4g
- Sodium: 900mg

Enjoy this delightful Goblin Gravy as you unravel mysteries and savor the essence of Scooby-Doo's culinary escapades!

82. Phantom Pesto Pasta

Embark on a culinary adventure with the Mystery Inc. gang as we unveil the secrets of the "Phantom Pesto Pasta." Inspired by the sleuthing escapades of Scooby-Doo and his friends, this pasta dish is a mysterious medley of flavors that will keep you guessing until the last bite. Unravel the enigma of this delightful meal, perfect for fans of all ages!

Serving: 4 servings
Preparation Time: 15 minutes

Ready Time: 25 minutes

Ingredients:
- 1 pound (450g) spaghetti
- 2 cups fresh basil leaves, packed
- 1/2 cup grated Parmesan cheese
- 1/2 cup pine nuts, toasted
- 3 cloves garlic
- 1/2 cup extra-virgin olive oil
- Salt and pepper to taste
- 1 cup cherry tomatoes, halved
- 1/2 cup black olives, sliced
- 1/4 cup feta cheese, crumbled
- Optional: Red pepper flakes for heat

Instructions:
1. Prepare the Pasta:
- Cook the spaghetti according to package instructions until al dente.
- Drain the pasta and set aside.
2. Create the Phantom Pesto:
- In a food processor, combine the fresh basil, Parmesan cheese, toasted pine nuts, and garlic cloves.
- Pulse until the ingredients are finely chopped.
- With the processor running, slowly drizzle in the olive oil until the mixture forms a smooth pesto.
- Season with salt and pepper to taste.
3. Combine Pasta and Pesto:
- Toss the cooked spaghetti with the prepared pesto, ensuring the pasta is evenly coated.
4. Add Toppings:
- Gently fold in the halved cherry tomatoes and sliced black olives, distributing them evenly throughout the pasta.
5. Serve:
- Plate the Phantom Pesto Pasta and sprinkle crumbled feta cheese on top.
- For an extra kick, add red pepper flakes if desired.
6. Enjoy the Mystery Unveiled:
- Dive into the mysterious world of flavors as you savor each bite of the Phantom Pesto Pasta.

- Be prepared for a taste sensation that even Scooby-Doo would approve of!

Nutrition Information:
Note: Nutritional values are approximate and may vary based on specific ingredients and serving sizes.
- Calories: 480 per serving
- Total Fat: 28g
- Saturated Fat: 6g
- Trans Fat: 0g
- Cholesterol: 15mg
- Sodium: 350mg
- Total Carbohydrates: 45g
- Dietary Fiber: 4g
- Sugars: 2g
- Protein: 12g

Delight in the culinary mystery of the Phantom Pesto Pasta, a dish that captures the essence of Scooby-Doo's adventures in every forkful.

83. Shaggy's Sweet Potato Fries

Step into the world of mystery and munchies with Shaggy's Sweet Potato Fries! Inspired by everyone's favorite laid-back detective from Scooby-Doo, these fries are the perfect snack for your next sleuthing adventure. Packed with flavor and a hint of Shaggy's signature appetite, these sweet potato fries are sure to satisfy your cravings.

Serving: 4 servings
Preparation Time: 15 minutes
Ready Time: 35 minutes

Ingredients:
- 4 medium-sized sweet potatoes, peeled and cut into fries
- 2 tablespoons olive oil
- 1 teaspoon garlic powder
- 1 teaspoon onion powder
- 1 teaspoon paprika
- 1/2 teaspoon cumin

- 1/2 teaspoon salt (adjust to taste)
- 1/4 teaspoon black pepper
- 2 tablespoons cornstarch
- Cooking spray (for baking)

Instructions:
1. Preheat the Oven:
- Preheat your oven to 425°F (220°C).
2. Prepare the Sweet Potatoes:
- Peel the sweet potatoes and cut them into fry-shaped pieces.
3. Coat with Cornstarch:
- In a large bowl, toss the sweet potato fries with cornstarch until they are evenly coated. This will help make them crispy when baked.
4. Season the Fries:
- Drizzle the olive oil over the sweet potatoes and sprinkle with garlic powder, onion powder, paprika, cumin, salt, and black pepper. Toss well to ensure the fries are evenly coated with the seasonings.
5. Arrange on Baking Sheet:
- Line a baking sheet with parchment paper and arrange the seasoned sweet potato fries in a single layer, ensuring they are not crowded. This allows them to crisp up while baking.
6. Bake in the Oven:
- Bake in the preheated oven for 25-30 minutes, flipping the fries halfway through, until they are golden brown and crispy.
7. Serve Hot:
- Once baked, remove the sweet potato fries from the oven and let them cool for a few minutes. Serve hot and enjoy the deliciousness inspired by Shaggy and Scooby's favorite snacks!

Nutrition Information:
- *Note: Nutrition information is approximate and may vary based on specific ingredients used.*
- *Calories per serving: 220*
- *Total Fat: 7g*
- *Saturated Fat: 1g*
- *Cholesterol: 0mg*
- *Sodium: 350mg*
- *Total Carbohydrates: 38g*
- *Dietary Fiber: 6g*
- *Total Sugars: 8g*

- *Protein: 3g*

Get ready to solve mysteries with a plate full of Shaggy's Sweet Potato Fries!

84. Velma's Vanilla Yogurt Parfait

Indulge in the delightful world of Scooby-Doo with Velma's Vanilla Yogurt Parfait, a wholesome and scrumptious treat inspired by the brains behind Mystery Inc. This parfait is a perfect blend of creamy vanilla yogurt, crunchy granola, and fresh fruits – a combination that's as clever as Velma herself. Whether you're solving mysteries or satisfying your sweet tooth, this recipe is sure to be a hit.

Serving: Serves 4
Preparation Time: 15 minutes
Ready Time: 15 minutes

Ingredients:
- 2 cups vanilla yogurt
- 1 cup granola
- 1 cup mixed berries (strawberries, blueberries, raspberries)
- 1 banana, sliced
- 1/4 cup honey
- 1/4 cup chopped nuts (almonds, walnuts, or your choice)
- Fresh mint leaves for garnish (optional)

Instructions:
1. Layering the Base:
Begin by spooning a layer of vanilla yogurt into the bottom of each serving glass or bowl. Ensure an even distribution for a balanced parfait.
2. Adding the Crunch:
Sprinkle a generous layer of granola on top of the yogurt. The granola provides a delightful crunch that complements the creamy texture of the yogurt.
3. Berry Bliss:
Scatter a handful of mixed berries over the granola layer. Use a combination of strawberries, blueberries, and raspberries for a burst of color and flavor.

4. Banana Elegance:
Place slices of fresh banana on top of the berries. The natural sweetness of bananas adds a delicious touch to the parfait.

5. Drizzle of Honey:
Drizzle honey over the entire parfait. The honey not only enhances the sweetness but also adds a touch of golden richness to the dish.

6. Nutty Finish:
Sprinkle chopped nuts over the parfait. This step adds a nutty dimension and a satisfying crunch to each bite.

7. Repeat the Layers:
Repeat the layering process until the serving glass or bowl is filled, finishing with a dollop of vanilla yogurt on top.

8. Garnish (Optional):
For an extra touch of freshness, garnish the parfait with a few mint leaves.

9. Serve and Enjoy:
Refrigerate the parfaits for at least 15 minutes to allow the flavors to meld. Serve chilled and savor the delightful layers of Velma's Vanilla Yogurt Parfait.

Nutrition Information:
(Per Serving)
- Calories: 300
- Protein: 8g
- Carbohydrates: 45g
- Fiber: 5g
- Sugars: 28g
- Fat: 10g
- Saturated Fat: 3g
- Cholesterol: 15mg
- Sodium: 80mg

Note: Nutrition information is approximate and may vary based on specific ingredients used.

85. Daphne's Dill Pickle Spears

Scooby-Doo and his gang have embarked on countless mysteries, but one thing that always brings them together is their love for snacks!

Daphne's Dill Pickle Spears are a crunchy and tangy treat that would make the perfect addition to any sleuthing adventure. These pickles are not only delicious but also a nostalgic nod to the iconic Scooby-Doo series. Get ready to snack like a detective with this simple and tasty recipe!

Serving: 4 servings
Preparation Time: 15 minutes
Ready Time: 24 hours (for pickling)

Ingredients:
- 10 large pickling cucumbers, washed and cut into spears
- 2 cups white vinegar
- 2 cups water
- 3 tablespoons pickling salt
- 2 tablespoons sugar
- 2 teaspoons dill seeds
- 1 teaspoon black peppercorns
- 4 cloves garlic, peeled and smashed
- 1 teaspoon mustard seeds
- 1/2 teaspoon red pepper flakes (optional, for some heat)

Instructions:
1. In a large saucepan, combine the white vinegar, water, pickling salt, and sugar. Bring the mixture to a boil, stirring until the salt and sugar dissolve. Remove from heat and let it cool to room temperature.
2. In each clean jar, place a few dill seeds, black peppercorns, smashed garlic cloves, mustard seeds, and red pepper flakes if you like a bit of heat.
3. Pack the cucumber spears tightly into the jars, leaving about 1/2 inch of space at the top.
4. Pour the cooled brine over the cucumbers, ensuring they are completely submerged. Tap the jars gently to remove any air bubbles.
5. Seal the jars tightly and refrigerate for at least 24 hours to allow the flavors to meld.
6. Once pickled, Daphne's Dill Pickle Spears are ready to be enjoyed! Serve them as a snack on their own or alongside your favorite Scooby-Doo-inspired treats.

Nutrition Information:

(Per Serving)
- Calories: 35
- Total Fat: 0g
- Saturated Fat: 0g
- Cholesterol: 0mg
- Sodium: 1760mg
- Total Carbohydrates: 7g
- Dietary Fiber: 2g
- Sugars: 3g
- Protein: 1g

Note: Nutrition information is approximate and may vary based on specific ingredients used.

86. Fred's Fiesta Quesadillas

Embark on a culinary adventure inspired by Scooby-Doo with Fred's Fiesta Quesadillas! These zesty quesadillas are a tribute to Fred's love for solving mysteries and indulging in delicious meals. Packed with vibrant flavors and easy to prepare, they're perfect for any gathering or a quick, satisfying meal. Join Scooby and the gang as you whip up these Fred-approved Fiesta Quesadillas.

Serving: Makes 4 quesadillas
Preparation Time: 15 minutes
Ready Time: 25 minutes

Ingredients:
- 8 flour tortillas
- 2 cups cooked chicken, shredded
- 1 cup cheddar cheese, shredded
- 1 cup Monterey Jack cheese, shredded
- 1 cup corn kernels (fresh or frozen)
- 1/2 cup black beans, drained and rinsed
- 1/2 cup red bell pepper, diced
- 1/4 cup green onions, thinly sliced
- 1/4 cup fresh cilantro, chopped
- 1 teaspoon ground cumin
- 1 teaspoon chili powder

- 1/2 teaspoon garlic powder
- Salt and pepper to taste
- Cooking spray

Instructions:
1. In a large mixing bowl, combine the shredded chicken, cheddar cheese, Monterey Jack cheese, corn, black beans, red bell pepper, green onions, cilantro, ground cumin, chili powder, garlic powder, salt, and pepper. Mix well to ensure even distribution of ingredients.
2. Place four tortillas on a flat surface. Divide the chicken and vegetable mixture evenly among the tortillas, spreading it over one half of each tortilla.
3. Fold the empty half of each tortilla over the filling, creating a half-moon shape.
4. Heat a large skillet or griddle over medium heat and lightly coat with cooking spray.
5. Place the quesadillas on the skillet and cook for 2-3 minutes on each side or until the tortillas are golden brown and the cheese is melted.
6. Remove the quesadillas from the skillet and let them cool for a minute before slicing each into wedges.
7. Serve the quesadillas warm, with your favorite salsa, guacamole, or sour cream on the side.

Nutrition Information:
(Per Serving)
- Calories: 450
- Total Fat: 20g
- Saturated Fat: 10g
- Trans Fat: 0g
- Cholesterol: 80mg
- Sodium: 600mg
- Total Carbohydrates: 40g
- Dietary Fiber: 5g
- Sugars: 2g
- Protein: 28g

Note: Nutrition information is approximate and may vary based on specific ingredients and serving sizes.

87. Haunted Honeydew Skewers

Step into the mysterious world of Scooby-Doo with these "Haunted Honeydew Skewers," a delightful treat that combines the sweetness of honeydew with a touch of spookiness. Inspired by the countless haunted mansions and eerie landscapes our favorite mystery-solving gang encounters, these skewers are sure to add a playful and delicious element to your Scooby-Doo-themed gathering. Perfect for a snack or party appetizer, these Haunted Honeydew Skewers will have everyone exclaiming, "Zoinks, these are good!"

Serving: Makes approximately 12 skewers
Preparation Time: 15 minutes
Ready Time: 30 minutes

Ingredients:
- 1 medium-sized honeydew melon
- 1 cup seedless red grapes
- 1 cup blackberries
- 12 wooden skewers
- 1 tablespoon honey (for drizzling)
- 1 teaspoon lemon juice

Instructions:
1. Prepare the Ingredients:
- Peel the honeydew melon and cut it into bite-sized cubes.
- Wash the red grapes and blackberries.
- If using wooden skewers, soak them in water for about 10 minutes to prevent them from splintering.
2. Assemble the Skewers:
- Thread the honeydew cubes, red grapes, and blackberries onto the skewers in a spooky and random order, creating a colorful pattern reminiscent of Scooby-Doo's adventures.
3. Drizzle with Honey and Lemon:
- In a small bowl, mix together the honey and lemon juice.
- Drizzle the honey and lemon mixture over the assembled skewers for a touch of sweetness and citrusy brightness.
4. Chill:
- Place the skewers in the refrigerator for at least 15 minutes to chill and enhance the flavors.

5. Serve:
- Arrange the Haunted Honeydew Skewers on a serving platter and present them with a sense of mystery and fun. They are now ready to be enjoyed by your fellow mystery solvers!

Nutrition Information:
(Per Serving)
- Calories: 60 kcal
- Total Fat: 0.2g
- Cholesterol: 0mg
- Sodium: 1mg
- Total Carbohydrates: 15g
- Dietary Fiber: 2g
- Sugars: 10g
- Protein: 1g

These Haunted Honeydew Skewers are a playful and healthy addition to your Scooby-Doo-inspired menu, making them a hit with both kids and adults. Enjoy the mysterious and delicious flavors as you embark on your own culinary mystery-solving adventure!

88. Creepy Cauliflower Bites

Step into the mysterious world of Scooby-Doo with these "Creepy Cauliflower Bites"! Inspired by the quirky and spooky adventures of Mystery Inc., these cauliflower bites are not only delicious but also a fun and healthy snack for any Scooby-Doo fan. Perfect for gatherings, movie nights, or just when you're craving a snack with a touch of mystery.

Serving: Makes approximately 24 cauliflower bites.
Preparation Time: 15 minutes
Ready Time: 35 minutes

Ingredients:
- 1 large head of cauliflower, cut into florets
- 1 cup breadcrumbs
- 1/2 cup grated Parmesan cheese
- 1 teaspoon garlic powder
- 1 teaspoon onion powder

- 1/2 teaspoon smoked paprika
- 1/2 teaspoon salt
- 1/4 teaspoon black pepper
- 2 large eggs
- Cooking spray

Instructions:

1. Preheat the Oven:
Preheat your oven to 400°F (200°C) and line a baking sheet with parchment paper.
2. Prepare the Cauliflower:
Cut the cauliflower into bite-sized florets, ensuring they are relatively uniform in size for even cooking.
3. Create the Coating Mixture:
In a bowl, combine the breadcrumbs, grated Parmesan cheese, garlic powder, onion powder, smoked paprika, salt, and black pepper. Mix well to ensure even distribution of flavors.
4. Coat the Cauliflower:
Dip each cauliflower floret into the beaten eggs, ensuring it is fully coated. Then, roll the cauliflower in the breadcrumb mixture, pressing gently to help the coating adhere.
5. Arrange on Baking Sheet:
Place the coated cauliflower bites on the prepared baking sheet, leaving some space between each piece to allow for even browning.
6. Bake to Perfection:
Bake in the preheated oven for 20-25 minutes or until the cauliflower is tender and the coating is golden brown and crispy.
7. Serve and Enjoy:
Once baked, remove from the oven and let them cool slightly. Serve your Creepy Cauliflower Bites with your favorite dipping sauce, and enjoy the mysterious flavor!

Nutrition Information:
- Serving Size: 4 cauliflower bites
- Calories: 120
- Total Fat: 4g
- Saturated Fat: 1.5g
- Cholesterol: 50mg
- Sodium: 320mg
- Total Carbohydrates: 16g

- Dietary Fiber: 3g
- Sugars: 2g
- Protein: 6g

Note: Nutrition information is approximate and may vary based on specific ingredients and serving sizes.

89. Ghostly Gorgonzola Dip

Step into the spooky world of Scooby-Doo with this delectable Ghostly Gorgonzola Dip. Inspired by the mysterious and thrilling adventures of Mystery Inc., this dip is sure to be a hit at your next gathering. Creamy gorgonzola cheese, blended with a hint of garlic and other savory ingredients, creates a hauntingly delicious flavor that will leave your taste buds craving more. Pair it with your favorite snacks for a snack that's both mysterious and mouthwatering.

Serving: This Ghostly Gorgonzola Dip serves 6-8 people.
Preparation Time: 15 minutes
Ready Time: 30 minutes

Ingredients:
- 8 oz gorgonzola cheese, crumbled
- 1 cup sour cream
- 1/2 cup mayonnaise
- 2 cloves garlic, minced
- 1 teaspoon Worcestershire sauce
- 1/2 teaspoon onion powder
- 1/2 teaspoon black pepper, freshly ground
- 1/4 cup fresh chives, chopped (for garnish)
- Assorted vegetables, crackers, or bread for dipping

Instructions:
1. In a medium-sized mixing bowl, combine the crumbled gorgonzola cheese, sour cream, mayonnaise, minced garlic, Worcestershire sauce, onion powder, and freshly ground black pepper.
2. Mix the ingredients thoroughly until well combined. Ensure that the gorgonzola is evenly distributed throughout the mixture.

3. Cover the bowl with plastic wrap and refrigerate the dip for at least 15 minutes. This allows the flavors to meld together and enhances the overall taste.
4. Before serving, garnish the Ghostly Gorgonzola Dip with freshly chopped chives for a burst of color and added freshness.
5. Arrange an assortment of vegetables, crackers, or bread around the dip for dipping. The dip pairs perfectly with carrot sticks, celery, cherry tomatoes, and crispy pita chips.
6. Serve the Ghostly Gorgonzola Dip at your Scooby-Doo-themed gathering and watch it disappear as mysteriously as the ghostly villains in the cartoon!

Nutrition Information:
(Per Serving - Based on 8 servings)
- Calories: 280
- Total Fat: 25g
- Saturated Fat: 12g
- Cholesterol: 55mg
- Sodium: 480mg
- Total Carbohydrates: 4g
- Dietary Fiber: 0g
- Sugars: 1g
- Protein: 9g

Enjoy the spooky goodness of this Ghostly Gorgonzola Dip as you embark on your own culinary adventure inspired by Scooby-Doo!

90. Werewolf Walnut Trail Mix

Unleash the mystery-solving appetite within with our Werewolf Walnut Trail Mix—a snack inspired by the legendary adventures of Scooby-Doo and the gang! Packed with the perfect combination of crunchy, savory, and slightly spooky elements, this trail mix is sure to fuel your taste buds on your own mysterious quests. Beware; you might find yourself howling for more!

Serving: 8 servings
Preparation time: 10 minutes
Ready time: 15 minutes

Ingredients:
- 1 cup walnuts, halved
- 1 cup pretzel twists
- 1 cup honey-flavored cereal squares
- 1/2 cup dried cranberries
- 1/2 cup dark chocolate chunks
- 1/2 cup mini marshmallows
- 1/4 cup shredded coconut, toasted
- 2 tablespoons maple syrup
- 1 tablespoon unsalted butter, melted
- 1/2 teaspoon cinnamon
- 1/4 teaspoon sea salt

Instructions:
1. Preheat your oven to 350°F (175°C).
2. In a large mixing bowl, combine the walnuts, pretzel twists, cereal squares, dried cranberries, dark chocolate chunks, mini marshmallows, and toasted shredded coconut.
3. In a small bowl, whisk together the maple syrup, melted butter, cinnamon, and sea salt until well combined.
4. Pour the maple syrup mixture over the dry ingredients in the large bowl. Toss everything together until the dry ingredients are evenly coated with the syrup mixture.
5. Spread the mixture evenly on a baking sheet lined with parchment paper.
6. Bake in the preheated oven for 10-12 minutes or until the mixture is golden brown, stirring halfway through to ensure even toasting.
7. Remove from the oven and let it cool completely.
8. Once cooled, break the trail mix into bite-sized clusters and transfer to an airtight container.

Nutrition Information (per serving):
- Calories: 240
- Total Fat: 14g
- Saturated Fat: 5g
- Trans Fat: 0g
- Cholesterol: 5mg
- Sodium: 140mg
- Total Carbohydrates: 28g

- Dietary Fiber: 3g
- Sugars: 14g
- Protein: 4g

Note: Nutrition information is approximate and may vary based on specific ingredients used. Adjustments can be made to cater to dietary preferences and restrictions. Enjoy your Werewolf Walnut Trail Mix on your next Scooby-Doo marathon or outdoor adventure!

91. Mummy Mango Smoothie

Get ready to embark on a delicious mystery-solving adventure with our "Mummy Mango Smoothie," inspired by the iconic Scooby-Doo and the gang! This refreshing smoothie is not only a tasty treat but also a sneaky way to enjoy the goodness of fruits. Perfect for breakfast or as a mid-day snack, it's a recipe that will have you saying, "Scooby-Dooby-Doo, where are you?" in no time!

Serving: 2 servings
Preparation Time: 10 minutes
Ready Time: 10 minutes

Ingredients:
- 2 ripe mangoes, peeled and diced
- 1 banana, peeled
- 1 cup Greek yogurt
- 1/2 cup orange juice
- 1/2 cup milk
- 1 tablespoon honey
- 1/2 teaspoon vanilla extract
- Ice cubes (optional)

Instructions:
1. In a blender, combine the diced mangoes, banana, Greek yogurt, orange juice, milk, honey, and vanilla extract.
2. Blend the ingredients on high speed until smooth and creamy. If you prefer a thicker consistency, you can add ice cubes and blend again.
3. Taste the smoothie and adjust the sweetness by adding more honey if needed.

4. Pour the Mummy Mango Smoothie into glasses.
5. Optional: Garnish with mango slices or a banana slice on the rim for a fun, spooky touch.
6. Serve immediately and enjoy your mystery-solving treat!

Nutrition Information:
(Per serving)
- Calories: 220 kcal
- Protein: 8g
- Carbohydrates: 45g
- Fiber: 4g
- Sugars: 32g
- Fat: 2g
- Saturated Fat: 1g
- Cholesterol: 5mg
- Sodium: 35mg
- Potassium: 630mg
- Vitamin C: 70mg
- Calcium: 150mg
- Iron: 1mg

Unmask the flavor in this delightful Mummy Mango Smoothie, a Scooby-Doo-inspired creation that combines the sweetness of mangoes with the creaminess of yogurt for a chillingly good treat!

92. Frankenberry French Toast

Embark on a culinary adventure inspired by the mystery-solving antics of Scooby-Doo and his gang with our delightful "Frankenberry French Toast" recipe. This whimsical dish pays homage to the iconic Scooby-Doo villain, Frankenberry, with a playful twist on classic French toast. Perfect for breakfast or brunch, this recipe is sure to awaken your taste buds and leave you ready for the next mystery!

Serving: Serves 4
Preparation Time: 15 minutes
Ready Time: 25 minutes

Ingredients:

- 8 slices of thick-cut bread (brioche or challah works well)
- 4 large eggs
- 1 cup milk
- 1 teaspoon vanilla extract
- 1/2 teaspoon cinnamon
- Pinch of salt
- 1 cup crushed Frankenberry cereal
- Butter, for cooking
- Whipped cream, for serving (optional)
- Fresh berries, for garnish (optional)
- Maple syrup, for drizzling

Instructions:
1. Prepare the Batter:
In a large mixing bowl, whisk together the eggs, milk, vanilla extract, cinnamon, and a pinch of salt until well combined. This will be your flavorful batter for the French toast.
2. Crush the Frankenberry Cereal:
Place the Frankenberry cereal in a sealable plastic bag and crush it with a rolling pin or the back of a spoon until you have a coarse crumb texture. Set aside in a shallow dish.
3. Dip and Coat:
Dip each slice of bread into the prepared batter, making sure to coat both sides evenly. Allow any excess batter to drip off.
4. Coat with Frankenberry Crumbs:
After dipping the bread in the batter, press each side into the crushed Frankenberry cereal, ensuring a generous coating adheres to the bread.
5. Cook the French Toast:
In a large skillet or griddle, melt butter over medium heat. Cook each slice of coated bread for 2-3 minutes per side or until golden brown and crispy.
6. Serve:
Place the Frankenberry French Toast on a serving plate. Top with a dollop of whipped cream, fresh berries, and a drizzle of maple syrup if desired.

Nutrition Information:
(Per Serving)
- Calories: 350
- Total Fat: 12g

- Saturated Fat: 5g
- Cholesterol: 185mg
- Sodium: 400mg
- Total Carbohydrates: 48g
- Dietary Fiber: 2g
- Sugars: 18g
- Protein: 12g

Note: Nutrition information is approximate and may vary based on specific ingredients and portion sizes.

Enjoy your Frankenberry French Toast, a delicious and nostalgic treat that brings the spirit of Scooby-Doo to your breakfast table!

93. Zombie Zoodle Stir-Fry

Step into the spooky and mysterious world of Scooby-Doo with our ghoulishly delicious "Zombie Zoodle Stir-Fry"! Inspired by the thrilling adventures of Scooby and the gang, this dish is not only fun but also a healthy and satisfying way to fuel your appetite. Packed with colorful veggies and zesty flavors, it's a meal that's sure to solve any hunger mystery.

Serving: 4 servings
Preparation Time: 15 minutes
Ready Time: 25 minutes

Ingredients:
- 2 zucchinis, spiralized into zoodles
- 1 cup broccoli florets
- 1 red bell pepper, thinly sliced
- 1 yellow bell pepper, thinly sliced
- 1 cup snap peas, trimmed
- 1 carrot, julienned
- 1 cup shredded cabbage
- 2 tablespoons vegetable oil
- 3 cloves garlic, minced
- 1 tablespoon ginger, grated
- 1 lb cooked chicken breast, sliced (optional for non-vegetarian version)
- 3 tablespoons soy sauce

- 1 tablespoon hoisin sauce
- 1 teaspoon sesame oil
- 1 teaspoon Sriracha sauce (adjust to taste)
- Sesame seeds for garnish
- Chopped green onions for garnish

Instructions:
1. Heat vegetable oil in a large wok or skillet over medium-high heat.
2. Add minced garlic and grated ginger, sauté for 1-2 minutes until fragrant.
3. Add broccoli, bell peppers, snap peas, carrot, and shredded cabbage to the wok. Stir-fry for 3-5 minutes until vegetables are tender-crisp.
4. If using chicken, add the sliced cooked chicken to the vegetables and stir to combine.
5. Push the vegetables and chicken (if used) to one side of the wok. On the other side, add the zucchini noodles and stir-fry for 2-3 minutes until just tender.
6. Combine the zoodles with the vegetable and chicken mixture in the wok.
7. In a small bowl, mix soy sauce, hoisin sauce, sesame oil, and Sriracha. Pour the sauce over the stir-fry and toss everything together until well coated.
8. Cook for an additional 2-3 minutes until the entire dish is heated through.
9. Garnish with sesame seeds and chopped green onions before serving.

Nutrition Information (per serving):
- Calories: 250
- Protein: 20g
- Carbohydrates: 20g
- Fat: 10g
- Fiber: 5g
- Sugar: 8g
- Sodium: 800mg

Note: Nutrition information is approximate and may vary based on specific ingredients used. Adjust quantities and ingredients as needed to meet dietary preferences.

94. Vampire Vanilla Pudding

Step into the spooky world of Scooby-Doo with this enchanting treat – Vampire Vanilla Pudding. Inspired by the mysterious and thrilling adventures of Mystery Inc., this dessert is sure to satisfy your sweet tooth with a touch of eerie delight. Creamy vanilla goodness meets the allure of the supernatural in every spoonful, making it a bewitching addition to your Scooby-Doo-inspired culinary journey.

Serving: 4 servings
Preparation Time: 15 minutes
Ready Time: 2 hours (including chilling time)

Ingredients:
- 2 cups whole milk
- 1/2 cup granulated sugar
- 1/4 cup cornstarch
- 1/4 teaspoon salt
- 4 large egg yolks
- 2 tablespoons unsalted butter
- 2 teaspoons pure vanilla extract
- Red gel food coloring
- Chocolate shavings or cookie crumbs for garnish (optional)

Instructions:
1. Prepare the Base:
In a medium saucepan, whisk together the sugar, cornstarch, and salt. In a separate bowl, whisk together the egg yolks and 1/2 cup of the milk until well combined.
2. Cook the Pudding Mixture:
Gradually whisk the egg mixture into the dry ingredients in the saucepan. Place the saucepan over medium heat and gradually whisk in the remaining milk. Cook the mixture, whisking constantly, until it thickens and comes to a gentle boil. This should take about 8-10 minutes.
3. Incorporate Butter and Vanilla:
Remove the saucepan from heat and stir in the butter and vanilla extract until the butter is melted and the vanilla is well distributed.
4. Create the Vampire Hue:

Add a few drops of red gel food coloring to the pudding mixture, stirring until you achieve a deep, vampire-worthy red hue. Adjust the color according to your preference.

5. Chill the Pudding:

Pour the pudding into individual serving bowls or glasses. Cover with plastic wrap, ensuring the wrap touches the surface of the pudding to prevent a skin from forming. Chill in the refrigerator for at least 2 hours or until set.

6. Garnish and Serve:

Before serving, add a sprinkle of chocolate shavings or cookie crumbs on top for an extra touch of mystery and texture. Unveil the Vampire Vanilla Pudding to your guests and watch them be delighted by this spooky yet scrumptious treat.

Nutrition Information:
(Per serving)
- Calories: 280
- Total Fat: 12g
- Saturated Fat: 7g
- Trans Fat: 0g
- Cholesterol: 215mg
- Sodium: 140mg
- Total Carbohydrates: 35g
- Dietary Fiber: 0g
- Sugars: 28g
- Protein: 7g

Delight in the magic of Scooby-Doo with this Vampire Vanilla Pudding – a dessert that brings a taste of the supernatural to your table. Enjoy the mysterious flavor and share it with your favorite gang of friends!

95. Goblin Garlic Knots

Embark on a culinary adventure with these whimsically named "Goblin Garlic Knots," inspired by the mysterious and mischievous world of Scooby-Doo. These savory knots are not only a treat for your taste buds but also a nod to the fantastical creatures that the Mystery Inc. gang encounters on their thrilling escapades. Whip up a batch of these garlicky delights and transport yourself to the heart of a Scooby-Doo mystery!

Serving: 4-6 people
Preparation Time: 15 minutes
Ready Time: 1 hour (including rising time)

Ingredients:
- 1 pound pizza dough, store-bought or homemade
- 1/2 cup unsalted butter, melted
- 4 cloves garlic, minced
- 2 tablespoons fresh parsley, finely chopped
- 1/2 cup grated Parmesan cheese
- Salt, to taste

Instructions:
1. Preheat and Prepare:
Preheat your oven to 375°F (190°C). Line a baking sheet with parchment paper.
2. Divide and Roll:
Divide the pizza dough into golf ball-sized portions. Roll each portion into a rope, about 8 inches long.
3. Create Knots:
Tie each rope into a simple knot, tucking the ends underneath. Place the knots on the prepared baking sheet, leaving some space between each.
4. Garlic Butter Mixture:
In a bowl, mix the melted butter, minced garlic, and a pinch of salt. Brush each garlic knot generously with the garlic butter mixture.
5. Bake to Perfection:
Bake in the preheated oven for 15-20 minutes or until the knots are golden brown and cooked through.
6. Garnish:
Remove the knots from the oven and immediately sprinkle them with chopped parsley and grated Parmesan cheese.
7. Serve Warm:
Allow the Goblin Garlic Knots to cool slightly before serving. These are best enjoyed warm, either on their own or as a side to your favorite Scooby-Doo inspired dish.

Nutrition Information (per serving):
(Note: Nutritional values are approximate and may vary based on specific ingredients and portion sizes.)

- Calories: 250 kcal
- Fat: 14g
- Saturated Fat: 8g
- Cholesterol: 30mg
- Sodium: 450mg
- Carbohydrates: 26g
- Fiber: 1g
- Sugar: 1g
- Protein: 5g

Unravel the mystery of flavor with these Goblin Garlic Knots, a delightful addition to your Scooby-Doo-inspired culinary journey!

96. Ghoulish Grilled Pineapple

Get ready to embark on a culinary adventure with our "Ghoulish Grilled Pineapple" recipe, inspired by the spooky and mysterious world of Scooby-Doo. This tantalizing treat combines the sweetness of pineapple with a hint of smokiness, creating a delightful snack or dessert that even the Mystery Inc. gang would approve of. Fire up the grill and let the ghoulish goodness begin!

Serving: Serves 4
Preparation Time: 15 minutes
Ready Time: 25 minutes

Ingredients:
- 1 large pineapple, peeled and cored
- 1/4 cup honey
- 2 tablespoons lime juice
- 1 teaspoon chili powder
- 1/2 teaspoon ground cinnamon
- Pinch of salt
- Fresh mint leaves for garnish (optional)
- Vanilla ice cream for serving (optional)

Instructions:
1. Preheat your grill to medium-high heat.
2. Slice the pineapple into rings, about 1/2-inch thick.

3. In a small bowl, whisk together the honey, lime juice, chili powder, ground cinnamon, and a pinch of salt to create the marinade.
4. Brush the pineapple slices generously with the marinade on both sides.
5. Place the pineapple slices on the preheated grill and cook for 2-3 minutes on each side, or until grill marks form and the pineapple caramelizes slightly.
6. Remove the grilled pineapple slices from the grill and arrange them on a serving platter.
7. Drizzle any remaining marinade over the grilled pineapple and garnish with fresh mint leaves if desired.
8. Serve the Ghoulish Grilled Pineapple on its own or with a scoop of vanilla ice cream for an extra indulgent treat.

Nutrition Information:
(Per Serving)
- Calories: 150
- Total Fat: 0.5g
- Saturated Fat: 0g
- Cholesterol: 0mg
- Sodium: 50mg
- Total Carbohydrates: 40g
- Dietary Fiber: 3g
- Sugars: 30g
- Protein: 1g

Delight your taste buds with this Ghoulish Grilled Pineapple recipe, a perfect addition to your Scooby-Doo-inspired culinary journey!

97. Phantom Peach Cobbler

Step into the world of mystery and nostalgia with the Phantom Peach Cobbler, inspired by the beloved Scooby-Doo and the gang. This delightful dessert will transport you back to those thrilling adventures where solving mysteries was always accompanied by good food. Get ready to embark on a culinary journey filled with the essence of Scooby-Doo and the irresistible flavors of this peach cobbler.

Serving: 6-8 servings
Preparation Time: 15 minutes

Ready Time: 50 minutes

Ingredients:
- 6 cups fresh or canned peaches, peeled and sliced
- 1 cup granulated sugar
- 1/4 cup brown sugar
- 1/4 cup unsalted butter
- 1 tablespoon lemon juice
- 1 teaspoon vanilla extract
- 1 cup all-purpose flour
- 1 cup milk
- 2 teaspoons baking powder
- 1/2 teaspoon salt
- 1/2 teaspoon ground cinnamon
- Whipped cream or vanilla ice cream (optional, for serving)

Instructions:
1. Preheat the Oven:
Preheat your oven to 375°F (190°C).
2. Prepare the Peaches:
If using fresh peaches, peel and slice them. If using canned peaches, drain them well. Place the sliced peaches in a large mixing bowl.
3. Sweeten the Peaches:
Add granulated sugar, brown sugar, lemon juice, and vanilla extract to the peaches. Stir gently until the peaches are well coated. Allow the mixture to sit for about 15 minutes to let the flavors meld.
4. Melt the Butter:
In a baking dish, melt the unsalted butter in the preheated oven.
5. Prepare the Batter:
In a separate bowl, whisk together the flour, milk, baking powder, salt, and ground cinnamon until you have a smooth batter.
6. Combine Ingredients:
Pour the batter over the melted butter in the baking dish, but do not stir. Spoon the sweetened peach mixture over the batter, distributing it evenly.
7. Bake:
Bake in the preheated oven for 40-45 minutes or until the top is golden brown and the cobbler is bubbling around the edges.
8. Serve:

Allow the Phantom Peach Cobbler to cool slightly before serving. Serve warm, and optionally, top with whipped cream or a scoop of vanilla ice cream for an extra treat.

Nutrition Information:
(Per Serving)
- Calories: 280
- Total Fat: 7g
- Saturated Fat: 4g
- Cholesterol: 20mg
- Sodium: 260mg
- Total Carbohydrates: 53g
- Dietary Fiber: 3g
- Sugars: 38g
- Protein: 3g

Indulge in this delightful Phantom Peach Cobbler and let the flavors transport you to a world of mystery and deliciousness. Enjoy the perfect blend of sweet peaches and warm cobbler—a recipe that captures the essence of Scooby-Doo's adventures!

98. Swampy Strawberry Salad

Get ready to embark on a culinary adventure inspired by the mystery-solving gang from Scooby-Doo! The "Swampy Strawberry Salad" is a delightful concoction that combines the freshness of strawberries with a touch of mystery, just like those eerie swamps the gang often finds themselves in. This salad is not only a treat for your taste buds but also a nod to the thrilling escapades of Scooby and the gang. Scooby-Dooby-Doo, where are you? Right here, savoring this delectable Swampy Strawberry Salad!

Serving: 4 servings
Preparation Time: 15 minutes
Ready Time: 15 minutes

Ingredients:
- 2 cups fresh strawberries, hulled and halved
- 1 cup cucumber, diced

- 1/2 cup red onion, finely sliced
- 1/4 cup feta cheese, crumbled
- 1/4 cup toasted pecans, chopped
- 1/4 cup fresh mint leaves, chopped

For the Swampy Strawberry Dressing:
- 2 tablespoons balsamic vinegar
- 1 tablespoon honey
- 2 tablespoons olive oil
- 1 teaspoon Dijon mustard
- Salt and pepper to taste

Instructions:
1. Prepare the Swampy Strawberry Dressing:
- In a small bowl, whisk together balsamic vinegar, honey, olive oil, Dijon mustard, salt, and pepper. Set aside.
2. Assemble the Salad:
- In a large bowl, combine fresh strawberries, diced cucumber, sliced red onion, crumbled feta cheese, chopped toasted pecans, and fresh mint leaves.
3. Drizzle with Dressing:
- Pour the prepared Swampy Strawberry Dressing over the salad ingredients.
4. Toss Gently:
- Toss the salad gently to ensure all ingredients are coated with the dressing.
5. Serve:
- Divide the Swampy Strawberry Salad among four plates and serve immediately.

Nutrition Information:
(Per serving)
- Calories: 180
- Total Fat: 12g
- Saturated Fat: 3g
- Trans Fat: 0g
- Cholesterol: 10mg
- Sodium: 150mg
- Total Carbohydrates: 18g
- Dietary Fiber: 4g
- Sugars: 12g

- Protein: 3g
- Vitamin D: 0mcg
- Calcium: 80mg
- Iron: 1mg
- Potassium: 230mg

Note: Nutrition information is approximate and may vary based on specific ingredients used.

99. Monster Macadamia Nut Cookies

Scooby-Doo and his gang have embarked on countless mysteries, and their adventures have inspired some deliciously mysterious treats. One such delight is the "Monster Macadamia Nut Cookies." These cookies are loaded with crunchy macadamia nuts, sweet white chocolate, and oats, creating a monster-sized treat that even Scooby and Shaggy would find irresistible. So, gather your gang and get ready to solve the mystery of the empty cookie jar with these scrumptious Monster Macadamia Nut Cookies!

Serving: 24 cookies
Preparation time: 15 minutes
Ready time: 30 minutes

Ingredients:
- 1 cup unsalted butter, softened
- 1 cup granulated sugar
- 1 cup brown sugar, packed
- 2 large eggs
- 1 teaspoon vanilla extract
- 2 cups all-purpose flour
- 1 teaspoon baking soda
- 1/2 teaspoon baking powder
- 1/2 teaspoon salt
- 2 cups old-fashioned oats
- 1 cup macadamia nuts, chopped
- 1 cup white chocolate chips

Instructions:

1. Preheat your oven to 350°F (175°C) and line a baking sheet with parchment paper.
2. In a large mixing bowl, cream together the softened butter, granulated sugar, and brown sugar until light and fluffy.
3. Add the eggs one at a time, beating well after each addition. Stir in the vanilla extract.
4. In a separate bowl, whisk together the flour, baking soda, baking powder, and salt.
5. Gradually add the dry ingredients to the wet ingredients, mixing until just combined.
6. Fold in the oats, chopped macadamia nuts, and white chocolate chips until evenly distributed throughout the dough.
7. Using a cookie scoop or spoon, drop rounded tablespoons of dough onto the prepared baking sheet, leaving some space between each cookie.
8. Bake in the preheated oven for 10-12 minutes or until the edges are golden brown. The centers may still appear slightly soft.
9. Allow the cookies to cool on the baking sheet for 5 minutes before transferring them to a wire rack to cool completely.

Nutrition Information (per cookie):
- Calories: 240
- Total Fat: 14g
- Saturated Fat: 7g
- Trans Fat: 0g
- Cholesterol: 35mg
- Sodium: 110mg
- Total Carbohydrates: 27g
- Dietary Fiber: 2g
- Sugars: 16g
- Protein: 3g

These Monster Macadamia Nut Cookies are a perfect blend of sweetness and crunch, making them a delightful treat for any Scooby-Doo fan or cookie lover. Enjoy them with a glass of milk, and let the mystery-solving adventures continue!

100. Shiver-inducing Shrimp Cocktail

Get ready to embark on a culinary adventure with Scooby-Doo and the gang! Our "Shiver-inducing Shrimp Cocktail" is a tantalizing treat that will transport you to the mysterious and thrilling world of Scooby-Doo. This dish is not only a feast for your taste buds but also a nod to the spine-tingling moments the gang encounters during their investigations. So, gather your Scooby snacks and prepare to dive into a bowl of flavorful excitement!

Serving: 4 servings
Preparation Time: 15 minutes
Ready Time: 30 minutes

Ingredients:
- 1 pound large shrimp, peeled and deveined
- 1 cup cocktail sauce
- 2 tablespoons freshly squeezed lemon juice
- 1 teaspoon Worcestershire sauce
- 1 teaspoon hot sauce (adjust to taste)
- 1/2 teaspoon horseradish (optional for extra kick)
- 1/4 teaspoon black pepper, freshly ground
- 1/4 teaspoon salt
- 1/4 cup fresh cilantro, chopped (for garnish)
- Ice cubes (for serving)

Instructions:
1. Prepare the Shrimp: In a large pot, bring water to a boil. Add a pinch of salt and the peeled, deveined shrimp. Boil for 2-3 minutes or until the shrimp turn pink and opaque. Drain and immediately transfer the shrimp to a bowl of ice water to stop the cooking process. Once cooled, drain the shrimp.
2. Make the Cocktail Sauce: In a medium bowl, mix together the cocktail sauce, lemon juice, Worcestershire sauce, hot sauce, horseradish (if using), black pepper, and salt. Stir until well combined. Adjust the spice level to your liking.
3. Combine Shrimp and Sauce: Add the cooled shrimp to the cocktail sauce mixture. Toss gently to coat the shrimp evenly with the sauce.
4. Chill: Cover the bowl with plastic wrap and refrigerate for at least 15 minutes to allow the flavors to meld and the shrimp to chill.
5. Serve: When ready to serve, divide the shrimp and sauce among individual serving glasses or bowls. Garnish with chopped cilantro.

6. Presentation: For an extra Scooby-Doo touch, serve the shrimp cocktail over a bed of ice cubes to give it that shiver-inducing effect.

Nutrition Information:
(Per Serving)
- Calories: 180
- Protein: 25g
- Carbohydrates: 15g
- Fat: 2g
- Saturated Fat: 0.5g
- Cholesterol: 180mg
- Sodium: 800mg
- Fiber: 1g
- Sugars: 10g

Note: Nutrition information is approximate and may vary based on specific ingredients and portion sizes. Adjust quantities and measurements as needed to meet dietary preferences and restrictions.

101. Witches' Walnut Pesto

Step into the mysterious world of Scooby-Doo and his gang with this bewitching culinary creation - Witches' Walnut Pesto. Inspired by the spooky adventures and delightful camaraderie of Mystery Inc., this pesto is sure to enchant your taste buds with its rich flavors and intriguing blend of ingredients. Perfect for a Scooby-Doo-themed gathering or a spooky movie night, this Witches' Walnut Pesto is a delightful treat that even Scooby and Shaggy would approve of!

Serving: This recipe yields approximately 1 cup of Witches' Walnut Pesto, serving 4-6 people.
Preparation Time: 15 minutes
Ready Time: 15 minutes

Ingredients:
- 2 cups fresh basil leaves, packed
- 1/2 cup walnuts, toasted
- 1/2 cup grated Parmesan cheese
- 2 cloves garlic, peeled

- 1/2 cup extra-virgin olive oil
- 1/2 teaspoon salt
- 1/4 teaspoon black pepper
- 1/2 teaspoon lemon zest
- 1 tablespoon lemon juice
- 1/4 teaspoon red pepper flakes (optional, for extra heat)

Instructions:
1. In a food processor, combine the fresh basil, toasted walnuts, Parmesan cheese, and peeled garlic cloves.
2. Pulse the ingredients until coarsely chopped.
3. With the food processor running, slowly drizzle in the olive oil until the mixture forms a smooth paste.
4. Add salt, black pepper, lemon zest, and lemon juice. If you like a bit of heat, add red pepper flakes to taste.
5. Continue to process until all ingredients are well combined, and the pesto reaches your desired consistency.
6. Taste and adjust seasoning as needed.
7. Transfer the Witches' Walnut Pesto to a serving bowl.
8. Serve the pesto with your favorite pasta, spread it on toasted bread, or use it as a dip for fresh veggies.

Nutrition Information:
(Per Serving - 2 tablespoons)
- Calories: 180
- Total Fat: 18g
- Saturated Fat: 3g
- Cholesterol: 5mg
- Sodium: 220mg
- Total Carbohydrates: 2g
- Dietary Fiber: 1g
- Sugars: 0g
- Protein: 4g

Note: Nutrition information is approximate and may vary based on specific ingredients used.

Embrace the Scooby-Doo spirit as you indulge in this Witches' Walnut Pesto, a spellbinding addition to your Scooby-Doo-inspired culinary journey!

102. Goblin Green Bean Almondine

Scooby-Doo and the gang have encountered numerous spooky creatures, but every mystery ends with a hearty meal. Inspired by their adventures, we present the "Goblin Green Bean Almondine" – a dish that captures the essence of both mystery and deliciousness. This savory concoction combines crisp green beans, toasted almonds, and a touch of magic to create a meal worthy of Scooby snacks!

Serving: 4 servings
Preparation Time: 15 minutes
Ready Time: 25 minutes

Ingredients:
- 1 pound fresh green beans, washed and trimmed
- 1/2 cup sliced almonds
- 2 tablespoons unsalted butter
- 2 cloves garlic, minced
- 1/4 teaspoon red pepper flakes (adjust to taste)
- Salt and pepper to taste
- 1 tablespoon lemon juice
- 1 teaspoon lemon zest
- 1/4 cup fresh parsley, chopped

Instructions:
1. Blanch the Green Beans:
- Bring a large pot of salted water to a boil. Add the green beans and cook for 2-3 minutes until they are bright green and slightly tender. Immediately transfer them to a bowl of ice water to stop the cooking process. Drain and set aside.
2. Toast the Almonds:
- In a dry skillet over medium heat, toast the sliced almonds until they become golden and fragrant. Stir frequently to avoid burning. Once toasted, transfer to a plate and set aside.
3. Cook the Green Beans:
- In the same skillet, melt the butter over medium heat. Add minced garlic and red pepper flakes, sautéing for 1-2 minutes until the garlic is fragrant.
4. Combine Ingredients:

- Add the blanched green beans to the skillet. Toss to coat them evenly in the garlic-infused butter. Season with salt and pepper to taste.

5. Finish and Serve:
- Squeeze lemon juice over the green beans and sprinkle lemon zest and toasted almonds on top. Toss everything together until well combined. Cook for an additional 2-3 minutes.

6. Garnish and Enjoy:
- Remove from heat, sprinkle fresh parsley over the Goblin Green Bean Almondine, and give it a final toss. Serve immediately and enjoy this mysterious and flavorful dish!

Nutrition Information:
Note: Nutritional values are approximate and may vary based on specific ingredients used.
- Calories: 150 per serving
- Protein: 4g
- Fat: 11g
- Carbohydrates: 12g
- Fiber: 5g
- Sugar: 4g
- Sodium: 120mg

Uncover the mystery behind the delectable Goblin Green Bean Almondine – a dish that's sure to vanish from plates faster than a ghost in the night!

103. Ectoplasmic Edamame Dip

Embark on a culinary adventure with the "103 Food Ideas Inspired by Scooby-Doo" cookbook! Uncover the mysteries of flavor with our Ectoplasmic Edamame Dip—a spooky yet scrumptious creation that pays homage to the beloved Scooby-Doo series. This ghoulishly good dip is perfect for sharing at gatherings or as a spooky snack for your next mystery-solving marathon.

Serving: Makes approximately 2 cups of dip
Preparation Time: 15 minutes
Ready Time: 20 minutes

Ingredients:
- 2 cups frozen edamame, shelled
- 1/4 cup tahini
- 2 cloves garlic, minced
- 2 tablespoons olive oil
- 1 tablespoon lemon juice
- 1 teaspoon cumin
- 1/2 teaspoon salt
- 1/4 teaspoon black pepper
- 1/4 teaspoon smoked paprika (for that extra ghostly kick)
- 2 tablespoons fresh parsley, chopped (for garnish)
- 1 tablespoon chives, finely chopped (for garnish)
- Carrot sticks, cucumber slices, or pita chips (for dipping)

Instructions:
1. Boil Edamame: In a medium-sized pot, bring water to a boil. Add the shelled edamame and cook for 3-5 minutes or until tender. Drain and set aside.
2. Blend Ingredients: In a food processor, combine the boiled edamame, tahini, minced garlic, olive oil, lemon juice, cumin, salt, black pepper, and smoked paprika. Blend until smooth and creamy.
3. Adjust Consistency: If the dip is too thick, you can add a little more olive oil or water until you reach your desired consistency. Blend again to incorporate.
4. Taste and Adjust Seasonings: Taste the dip and adjust the seasonings if needed. You can add more salt, lemon juice, or spices to suit your preferences.
5. Serve: Transfer the Ectoplasmic Edamame Dip to a serving bowl. Garnish with chopped parsley and chives for an eerie touch.
6. Prepare Dippers: Serve with carrot sticks, cucumber slices, or pita chips for a hauntingly good dipping experience.
7. Enjoy: Dive into the supernatural flavors of this dip while reliving your favorite Scooby-Doo moments.

Nutrition Information:
Note: Nutrition information is approximate and may vary based on specific ingredients used.
- Calories: 120 per 1/4 cup serving
- Total Fat: 8g
- Saturated Fat: 1g

- Cholesterol: 0mg
- Sodium: 200mg
- Total Carbohydrates: 9g
- Dietary Fiber: 4g
- Sugars: 1g
- Protein: 5g

Scooby and the gang would undoubtedly approve of this Ectoplasmic Edamame Dip—so go ahead, dive in, and let the flavors unravel!

CONCLUSION

In concluding our culinary journey through the cookbook "Mystery Munchies: 103 Wholesome Recipes Inspired by Scooby-Doo," we find ourselves immersed in a world where the joy of cooking intersects with the nostalgia of our favorite animated mystery-solving gang. With 103 delectable recipes that pay homage to the iconic Scooby-Doo and his friends, this cookbook has not only tantalized our taste buds but also stirred cherished memories of Saturday morning cartoons and the thrilling adventures of the Mystery Inc. team.

As we close the pages of this culinary treasure trove, it's impossible not to appreciate the creativity and ingenuity that went into translating the whimsical world of Scooby-Doo into delightful, real-world recipes. From Scooby Snacks to Shaggy's Sandwich Surprise, each dish captures the essence of the characters and the mysteries they unraveled, making every meal an adventure in itself.

One of the cookbook's standout features is its ability to cater to a wide range of palates and dietary preferences. Whether you're a carnivore like Fred, a vegetarian like Velma, or a sweet tooth like Daphne, "Mystery Munchies" ensures that there's something for everyone at the dining table. The recipes effortlessly blend wholesome ingredients with a dash of Scooby-Doo magic, encouraging families and friends to come together over delicious, home-cooked meals.

Beyond the kitchen, the cookbook serves as a gateway to foster a love for cooking among younger generations. The playful nature of the recipes and the familiar characters encourage children to join in the culinary fun, turning the kitchen into a place of creativity and bonding. Parents and guardians can share their own Scooby-Doo memories while passing down the joy of preparing and enjoying good food.

What sets "Mystery Munchies" apart is its attention to detail in capturing the essence of the Scooby-Doo universe. The recipes not only reflect the characters' personalities but also incorporate elements of the mysteries they solved. From the Ghoul's Gourmet Pizza inspired by haunted castles to the Haunted Swamp Smoothie reminiscent of eerie adventures, each dish transports us to the heart of a Scooby-Doo episode.

The cookbook also pays homage to the timeless themes of friendship, bravery, and teamwork that define the Scooby-Doo narrative. Just as the gang collaborated to unmask villains, readers are encouraged to gather their own group of culinary detectives to embark on a shared cooking adventure. The communal aspect of preparing these dishes adds an extra layer of enjoyment to the overall culinary experience.

In essence, "Mystery Munchies" is more than just a cookbook; it's a celebration of the enduring charm of Scooby-Doo and the joy of creating and savoring delicious meals. It's an invitation to rediscover the magic of childhood while enjoying wholesome, flavorful recipes that bring the beloved characters to life in our kitchens. As we bid farewell to the pages filled with gastronomic delights and cartoon-inspired creativity, we carry with us the warmth of shared meals, laughter, and the timeless appeal of Scooby-Doo – a delightful journey that transcends both the kitchen and the animated screen.